CHRISTIANITY AND EXISTENTIALISM

CHRISTIANITY AND EXISTENTIALISM

BY

J. M. SPIER

Translated with an Introduction and notes

by

DAVID HUGH FREEMAN

Assistant Professor of Philosophy
Wilson College

TRANSLATOR'S PREFACE

IN HIS BOOK, *An Introduction to Christian Philosophy,* Mr. Spier demonstrated his ability to give a compact exposition of the philosophy of Hermann Dooyeweerd.[1] And now within comparatively few pages, Mr. Spier exposits and criticizes Existentialism, a movement noted for its obscurity and verbosity. Mr. Spier's work is of an introductory nature and does not intend to give an exhaustive account. The merit of his clear exposition and criticism is for the reader to judge.

To understand Spier's critical evaluation of Existentialism fully, the reader should have some knowledge of the philosophical school of which Spier is a member. In the following *Introduction* I shall briefly summarize some important features of this school. Those interested in a more comprehensive introduction should consult the writings of Dooyeweerd and Spier's own *Introduction to Christian Philosophy.*

In translating I have tried to give an accurate literal rendering of the Dutch text. I wish to express my appreciation to Mr. Spier, for his willingness to read my manuscript; to Miss Sybil Chance, for her suggestions and assistance in proof reading; to Miss Gloria Ericson, for typing the manuscript; and to Dr. Samuel G. Craig, President of the Presbyterian and Reformed Publishing Company, for his interest in Christian philosophy.

DAVID HUGH FREEMAN
Assistant Professor of Philosophy, Wilson College

1953

[1] Professor Dooyeweerd is the founder of a new school of Christian philosophy. His monumental work in three volumes, *De Wijsbegeerte der Wetsidee,* is now being published in a revised four volume English translation under the title, *A New Critique of Theoretical Thought,* H. J. Paris, Amsterdam and the Presbyterian and Reformed Publishing Co., Phila.

TRANSLATOR'S INTRODUCTION:

MR. SPIER's criticism of Existentialism is based upon a philosophy with which the reader may desire to be familiar. Although impossible to discuss Spier's philosophy in detail within the scope of a few pages, we shall briefly indicate some of its main characteristics.

Spier is a member of a new school of Christian philosophy which has become associated primarily with the name of its founder, Hermann Dooyeweerd. The latter was originally under the influence of Neo-Kantian philosophy and Husserl's phenomenology. The discovery of what he considered to be an intrinsic connection between philosophy and religion signified a radical change in his thinking. As a result he sought to develop a philosophy that is essentially Christian in nature and not dependent upon a synthesis of Christian dogma and non-Christian philosophy. The central thesis of his new philosophy is that theoretical thought is based upon super-theoretical ideas. The strictest scientific thinking rests upon non-scientific foundations so that pure unprejudiced reason does not exist. No philosophy can claim theoretical autonomy, because *religion*[1] and science are intrinsically and necessarily connected. To assume the autonomy of theoretical thought without being aware of the religious character of this assumption is to be uncritical and dogmatic.

This central thesis is not stated dogmatically by Spier or Dooyeweerd, but both think themselves to be truly

[1] The term "religion" is not used here in its narrow sense, but simply designates the most basic commitment that a person makes with respect to whatever he considers to be his "God." Whether "God" is taken to be human "reason," "society," or Jesus Christ, this commitment concerning the origin of meaning, in this basic sense, is included in what Spier means by "religion."

vii

critical simply because they are aware of the religious pre-suppositions of their own philosophy. Dooyeweerd believes that in the first volume of his new *Critique of Theoretical Thought,* he has established to the satisfaction of any truly critical thinker, whatever his religious loyalties and commitments may be, that theoretical thought is not autonomous but rests upon and is guided by pre-theoretical or religious assumptions.[1] It is on the basis of this *Critique* that Spier feels justified in making use of his own beliefs in criticizing an opposing school of philosophy.

Spier admits that his philosophical starting point is religious, but maintains that his Christian philosophy is truly critical and not dogmatic. It is quite legitimate to ask how philosophy can be scientific and at the same time have a religious starting point. How can one conduct a philosophical argument which yields conclusions acceptable to every unprejudiced mind when these very conclusions are to the effect that every philosophical argument is prejudiced by a religious bias? How can a person whose thinking is conditioned by his extra theoretical faith hope to reach conclusions that must be acknowledged by those sharing a rival faith? The central thesis of this school of philosophy comes into sharper focus at this point. No one intends to deny the possibility of theoretical thought but only to question the dogma that theoretical thought is autonomous. Theoretical thought can discover that it rests on presuppositions which are non-theoretical. It can disclose what the nature of these presuppositions are, but it cannot establish the truth or falsity of their content, as their truth-value is a matter of faith. Proceeding from antithetical faiths, philosophers cannot convict each other by theoretical argument of the

[1] Cf. Dooyeweerd, *Reformatie en Scholastiek in der Wijsbegeerte,* Vol. 1, in which he seeks to show the religious motive of form and matter at work in the philosophy of the pre-Socratics and in Plato.

error of their faiths, but can disclose only the presence of faith.

Modern philosophy is uncritical insofar as it fails to recognize the religious character of its starting point: a faith in the ideal of science, or in the ideal of human personality.

For philosophical thought to be possible it must have certain necessary presuppositions which are not philosophical. In our everyday life we experience reality in an unbreakable coherence. Nothing exists by itself, everything is related to everything else. All the various aspects of reality which the special sciences distinguish and analyse actually are inseparable. Number does not exist independently of space, nor does space exist apart from motion. The aspect of motion in turn is not free from the organic vital aspect which coheres with the physical emotive aspect. And the latter is connected with the analytical, and this with the historical, linguistical, social, economic, esthetic, juridical, moral and faith aspects. The task of philosophy is to provide a theoretical insight into the coherence of the aspects of experience. And philosophical thought can comprehend the totality of the cosmos only if it acquires knowledge of the self. Self-knowledge is the key to philosophical understanding and the knowledge that we have of our self can not be the result of rational analysis, because rational analysis is itself a function of the self.

Self-knowledge rests upon a commitment which we must necessarily make on faith. It is not possible for reason to determine *what man is*. Before one can begin to philosophize about the nature of man, a choice is already made on the part of man. Man assumes at the outset the limits of his own existence. He assumes that his reason, for example, is not in need of any point of reference outside of itself in order to render reality intelligible. Or he can assume that his reason is derivative, created by God.

In other words, prior to any philosophical discussion, the philosopher, and every one else, decides whether or not he is going to consider himself to be a creature of a God Who has revealed Himself or whether he is going to consider *himself* as being divine in an absolute sense. If a philosopher believes that there is no point of reference outside of his own reason or analytical function, then he is actually proclaiming his own theoretical thought to be the *Archimedean* point in terms of which everything in the world is to be ultimately explained. This choice of the *origin* of all meaning is a religious act. It is religious because it concerns whatever a person believes to be ultimate. There is no rational way that one can arrive at the assumption that reason is created or not created.

The starting point of both Christian and non-Christian philosophy rests upon a subjective religious faith, a faith either in a transcendent God, or in an ἀρχή such as reason.[1]

Christian philosophy recognizes the fact that man must interpret himself in the light of the Bible. It is conscious of its religious motives and readily recognizes the doctrine of creation, the fall, and redemption in Christ as its basic religious presuppositions. The Christian philosopher accepts the revelation of the Bible, but this revelation does not solve any philosophical problem simply because revelation transcends philosophic thought.

Philosophy is not theology, but philosophy does have a necessary religious presupposition, a necessary apriori which transcends the immanent structure of philosophic thought. Every philosopher must raise a basic religious question which is answered by a pre-theoretical commitment or presupposition. He must answer the question, What is the origin and what is the totality of meaning

---

[1] All philosophy which seeks its basic religious starting point within the cosmos is referred to by Spier as "immanence-philosophy."

of our cosmos? And, What is the mutual relationship and coherence between the aspects of cosmic diversity?[1]

Philosophy is not religion but it is based on a religious commitment which is not subject to direct proof but is a matter of faith. This view of philosophy and religion appears to be an encroachment upon the objectivity of science and philosophy. But it is this very idea of objectivity which is the point in question in Spier's philosophy. Spier's criticism of Existentialism is consciously conditioned by his pre-theoretical commitment; nevertheless, it does not follow that Spier is necessarily being uncritical. The reader should reserve his final judgment on this important point until he has examined Dooyeweerd's critique of theoretical thought.

If we examine logical positivism, for example, perhaps we can gain a clearer insight into the difficulty which confronts anyone who thinks that he can remain neutral with respect to a religious commitment.

Positivists often express the desire to break through the wall that separates science and philosophy by insisting that philosophy abandon any other criterion of meaning than a scientific one. In other words, a positivist would have philosophy adopt the method of the new science or be branded as meaningless. The position of science is supposedly neutral with respect to any world picture or idea of totality. Science is supposedly free from any theory about reality. At least in its theoretical aspects it employs solely a formal mode of speech and is free from any commitment with respect to the nature of reality. It is pre-

---

[1] The aspects of cosmic diversity are those aspects which the sciences analyse: the numerical, spatial, physical, organic, psychical, analytical, historical, linguistical, societal, economic, esthetic, juridical, moral and faith aspects. Each of these aspects or modalities forms its own irreducible lawsphere which is internally sovereign, although unbreakably united with the remaining aspects, and together they constitute the *cosmic law-order*.

cisely this idea of neutrality that Spier is calling into question. Is such neutrality possible? It would make sense to speak of the autonomy of physics if physics could actually be contemplated theoretically, apart from all other forms of human experience. It is true that one may choose to interpret all forms of experience in terms of sense perception and may formulate a criterion of meaning which insists upon an empirical element, but is such an assumption free from a pre-theoretical commitment which is beyond the scope of a special science or philosophic thought?

It is a common doctrine of positivists that science can be unified by the elimination of metaphysics, for then one language or common denominator can be employed. Propositions are meaningful if they contain perception terms as predicates. Is this criterion of meaning really neutral? Is not this very criterion and would be neutrality a metaphysical commitment or more accurately a pre-theoretical religious commitment? For how can one defend the contention that "meaningful statements must have perception terms as predicates"? Is this "statement" scientific or metaphysical? If scientific then it must also have perception terms as its predicate. But the statement, "a meaningful statement is a statement which has a perception term as its predicate," is vague. Is the predicate of this statement a perception term? Or is it an intuitive term? If it is a mere convention, what guarantee is there that agreement will be reached by all scientists concerning its validity? In what sense is science objective? How will science be unified? Why must philosophy accept this convention?

It seems that any statement or presupposition which insists that all meaningful statements must contain a sense-term predicate is itself not meaningful. This would-be criterion of meaning is self contradictory, if taken as an axiom.

If it is only a postulate or a statement of our scientific faith, then its use would not be dogmatic. Then the formulation of this criterion of meaning would have to be restated to be: "*I believe* that meaningful statements consist exclusively of statements with sense-term predicates." Of course this admission would be an abandonment of any positivistic objection to metaphysics. A Hegelian could equally voice his faith in the Absolute Spirit. Spier contends that a criterion of meaning is necessarily the result of a pre-philosophic pre-theoretical commitment. Our initial starting point cannot be demonstrated by any direct proof. We must make a choice and this choice presupposes a view of our self, of the totality of the cosmos and its origin.

Consequently, it appears that the school of which Spier is a member has touched a real difficulty and is perhaps being truly scientific and critical in acknowledging that there is an intrinsic connection between philosophical thought and religious faith. It is for this reason that Spier feels justified in criticizing Existentialism from the standpoint of his own philosophy, which makes use of Christian motives.

Spier believes that philosophy is a science, but it is a science that is occupied with the entire temporal cosmos in such a way that the cosmos is viewed in relation to its origin.

The world which we experience is a created world. It is meaningful in relation to God. Each aspect of reality (i.e., number, space, motion, life, feeling, thinking, history, language, society, economy, beauty, law, love, and faith) are related to each other. The world is not irrationalistic, but has been created by God in such a way that everything is subject to the laws of God in a *cosmic-law-order*.

This terminates our brief outline of some of the main

points of Spier's own philosophy. We have given this introduction merely to enable the reader to follow Spier's method of criticism. To acquire a knowledge of this new Christian philosophy the reader is directed to the sources which have been mentioned.

DAVID HUGH FREEMAN

CONTENTS

INTRODUCTION

EXISTENTIALISM, to which the names of Heidegger, Jaspers, Sartre, and others are joined, is by no means an insignificant movement in contemporary philosophy. It is undoubtedly distinguished from other contemporary philosophical systems by an ever increasing degree of popularity.

The general public is refreshed in various ways by the wisdom and ideas of Existentialism. The notions of Existentialism are the common possession of many and exercise an influence upon modern Society's view of life and its tempo. As a result, modern life increasingly withdraws itself from the beneficial influence of Christianity.

The popularity of Existentialism is not due to the fact that its philosophical motives and ideals are so clear and intelligible that they can be easily comprehended by the masses. On the contrary, its constructions, and manner of expression are often obscure and difficult and require a great deal of effort. The reason for the great influence of Existentialism is that it is a philosophy of crisis. It attracts the contemporary man, by fortifying and appealing to his attitude toward life which is often characterized by doubt, despair, futility, and nihilism. Existentialism—at least in the case of its leading exponents—is a philosophy of the meaninglessness of life, of the nihility, and mortality of human existence which is devoid of any prospect or future.

The catastrophes of the twentieth century have caused the masses to lose faith in former values and ideals. Because of the chaotic cultural confusion of the last dicennia previously cherished ideals are now looked upon by the masses as illusions. For this reason the tenets of Existentialism find a point of contact and a ready audience.

Existentialism enlists the service of a radical and nihilistic attitude. Not only does it seek philosophically to describe and to account for such a mentality but it exalts this attitude, extolling it as the highest (temporal) form of wisdom and the only answer that can be given by man in a situation which is intrinsically desperate. Thus, this philosophy acquires for many the aureole of religion, a religion without God, a religion in apostasy.

In our contemporary life, Christianity encounters the highly successful phenomenon called Existentialism. How should it react? Christianity is not a living Christianity if it merely avoids its opponents and closes its eyes to a spiritual movement which by its doctrine holds many captive and causes them to enter into a dawnless night.

The desperate man of the twentieth century feels that he must accept with grim determination an existence which is without any future. Christianity has a message for our era and a task to perform. This message is the Gospel of Jesus Christ. And Christ speaks to modern man when He says: "I am the light of the world." This good news must be proclaimed in every sphere of life. It must be presented in all of its aspects to a generation which is frustrated in all its desires.

Christ said that all power in heaven and on earth is given to Him. Christianity, therefore, cannot neglect any aspect of life, but must seek to advance the Kingdom of God in all spheres, including that of Philosophy. It must oppose the kingdom of this world wherever it encounters the power of darkness, and in this struggle it need not fear to employ the weapons used by the children of the world.

Existentialism pretends that it has found an answer to the problems of modern man. We must examine this answer and seek to understand the spirit and problems of our time. The needs of our day are our needs. We are in the world and we must intensely participate in the development of human culture. We have a task to perform in philosophy and must test the spirit of the time to see if it is from God. We must measure it by the Word of God and reject as foolishness that which is not in harmony with God's Word, as it cannot give light to our times but only adds to the darkness.

Modern man is as a sheep without a shepherd. Caught in the throes of anxiety and despair, he wanders aimlessly and is ready to listen to false prophets. As true followers of Christ we ought to be moved to compassion for the multitude. We ought to give an answer which will illuminate the paths of those who wander in darkness, because such an answer is given in obedience to Him, Who said: "Whoever follows me shall not walk in darkness, but shall have the light of life."

As Christians our task is twofold. In the first place we must acquire a thorough knowledge of what Existentialism is. We must carefully study the systems of its foremost representatives in order to understand the spirit of our time. Understanding Existentialism, we shall be in a position to criticize it from a Biblical position; however, we shall see that our critique would be inadequate if we are merely negative and do not recognize the *moments of truth* which are present in this philosophy.

PART I

WHAT DOES THE PHILOSOPHY
OF EXISTENTIALISM TEACH?

PRELIMINARY SKETCH

It is not possible to give a simple answer to the question, "What does Existentialism teach?" Existentialism has many variations, its representatives being extremely diverse in their philosophical conceptions. Some existentialists seek to effect a positive synthesis with Christianity and others are extremely atheistic and nihilistic. A third group seeks to occupy an intermediary position. We cannot generalize but must examine each existentialist individually, but before we can fruitfully begin our examination we must investigate the background of this philosophy. Since every phenomenon of culture has its roots in the past, Existentialism has a philosophic and a non-philosophic background.

CHAPTER I

THE BACKGROUND OF EXISTENTIALISM

I

THE PHILOSOPHIC BACKGROUND

No philosophical system is entirely new; being historically determined, it is always related to the philosophic past, positively and negatively. Every school of thought forms a basis for future schools; no system speaks "the last word." Existentialism, being no exception, is also rooted in the past history of philosophy. Some of its motives are to be found in the Stoics and in Plotinus; but its main roots are to be found in modern Humanism.

Based upon the religious motives of "nature" and "freedom," modern Humanism possesses a passion to provide a philosophic foundation for *the ideal of a free and autonomous human personality.*[1]

The Post-Kantian philosophy of Fichte and Schelling culminated in the Absolute Idealism of Hegel *(Freiheits Idealisme).* The humanistic thought of Hegel viewed reality as the dialectical self-unfolding of Spirit, Idea, or Reason. The tendency after Kant had been to base the ideal of personality upon an irrationalistic speculative philosophy. Hegel discontinued this trend and by means

---

[1] For a full historical treatment of the motives of modern Humanism the reader should consult, H. Dooyeweerd, *A New Critique of Theoretical Thought,* Vol. I.

of dialectical logic rationalized the irrationalistic ideal of personality in a pan-logicism. Logical contradiction became a necessary stage in the dialectical process.[1]

Now, there is no direct line of development from Hegel to Existentialism. The relation between the two is antithetical. Existentialism is irrationalistic in character, and therefore cannot help but be opposed to the rationalism of Hegel; nevertheless, Existentialism is a Humanism. The antithesis between rationalism and irrationalism belongs solely within the cadre of humanistic philosophy. Humanism is committed to a philosophical faith in the autonomous freedom of human personality, and no matter how much the various representatives of Existentialism may differ among themselves, they all agree that man is absolutely autonomous. Nature can be dominated rationally, but man is completely free. In this connection S. U. Zuidema wrote: "The rationalistic conceptions of Humanism trusted solely in the exclusive redemptive power of *reason*. All existentialists are passionate in their opposition to this doctrine but they are equally vehement in their own confession of the autonomy of human freedom."[2]

We do not have time to give a complete sketch of the historical development, but our presentation would be completely inadequate if we failed to mention two thinkers who can be called the fathers of modern Existentialism. Let us pause, briefly, to examine these two men.

[1] H. Dooyeweerd, *De Wijsbegeerte der Wetsidee,* I pp. 371, 438 and 440.

[2] *Karacter van de moderne existentie-philosophie,* p. I.

II

KIERKEGAARD

Soren Kierkegaard was born in Copenhagen in 1813. He belonged to the Lutheran State Church but the influence of his father was extremely pietistic and it left a deep subjectivistic and individualistic impression upon the young Kierkegaard.

The life of Kierkegaard was a tragedy. From his father he inherited a melancholy disposition, a rich fantasy, and a tendency to engage in continual introspection. Kierkegaard studied theology but he never became a minister as he did not consider himself worthy and did not dare call himself a Christian even though he desired to be one. Instead he became a writer and devoted his pen to an attack on Hegel, whose philosophy he considered to be incompatible with Christianity. Although he was engaged to a girl whom he loved dearly, Kierkegaard never married, but broke the engagement as he did not consider himself worthy. This event was very painful to him and he never really recovered from it. The tragic in his life was further augmented by the mysterious confession of his father. Shortly before his death, Kierkegaard's father revealed the fact that in his youth he had once cursed God and human existence. Consequently, throughout his whole life he had been conscious of a Divine curse. Such a confession preyed upon the mind of the young Kierkegaard. He was conscious that he had escaped the curse but nevertheless it was a burden to him.

The last years of Kierkegaard's life were plagued by the persecutions of a local newspaper. He was deeply offended by the fact that the Church did not rise to his defense. He soon looked upon himself as a martyr of true

Christianity in contrast to the pseudo-Christianity of the Church. And shortly after, at the time of his death, he refused all Church ceremonies and consolations. Yet in spite of all the tragedy in his life Kierkegaard remained a faithful Christian. His last words expressed his confidence that he would soon enter into the eternal presence of the Lord Jesus.

The philosophic conceptions of Kierkegaard are not the product of a person who did not live in touch with life but are the result of personal struggles. Kierkegaard is the man of paradox. It is no wonder that his thinking is irrationalistic; he despised anything that was systematic. His concern was not with what is general and lawful but with what is individual and subjective. His whole attitude and convictions are anti-social. He considered society to be sinful in itself.

The individual was his only concern. Individual subjectivity alone is truth. To exist is to be with oneself alone before God. Anxiety about one's own personal salvation belongs to the very essence of faith (existential despair). Tension and conflict always exist in the relation between man and God because God is Holy, Exalted, and Unpredictable. He is completely Free, and bothered by no law. Man, in contrast, is sinful and small. The existential man, however, is also a man of freedom; he is not bound by any law. The official Christianity of the Church has become *bourgeois* and apostate. True Christianity is not the religion of the masses but of the *individual*, the martyr, the existential man. It is the religion of the existential man whose own freedom is in conflict with the freedom of God; that is, with the arbitrariness of God. Man flees from his own existence as soon as he subjects himself to laws and seeks certainty in universal rules. The thought of Kierkegaard is *individualistic* and *subjectivisitic*. Kierkegaard distinquished in human existence three ways to view

8

life. The first is the esthetic. This is the outlook of those who view life from a distance. It is the attitude of one who dispassionately observes and contemplates life as though he were himself not a part of it. Such a person is a rationalist and a positivist in his thought and in his deeds he seeks his own satisfaction. The second view of life is the ethical. In it man looks away from the external world and contemplates himself. He seeks to overcome his own guilt by finding fixed rules for his actions. Neither the esthetic nor the ethical is the true existential outlook. The latter is to be found solely in the *religious* form of life, which alone breaks all ties with the universal and with lawfulness. Only in it does the individual appear before God in his full freedom. In it alone is the individual confronted by the God-man, Christ who is the living paradox. In the religious outlook temporal man is confronted by God and stands before Him in despair and faith; and this *is to exist*. There is no gradual transition between these three outlooks toward life. The gaps between them are only bridged by a leap.

The idea of Kierkegaard that *existence* is the individual subjectivity of the free man has had a tremendous influence in all later Existentialism.

III

NIETZSCHE

AT FIRST glance it seems as though Kierkegaard and Nietzsche have nothing in common. The former, in spite of everything, remained a believing Christian whose foremost concern was the relation of man to God, while the latter is a self-avowed enemy of Christianity, a militant atheist who passionately disavowed and attacked its basic truths. Nevertheless, there is an inner connection between the conceptions of Kierkegaard and Nietzsche which enabled them to be forerunners of subsequent Existentialism. Both are irrationalists; they reject the supremacy of reason because they believe life to be more than rational thought. Their philosophy is more of a life and world view than a scientific system. Both are exclusively interested in man; for them philosophy is anthropology. Human existence is to exist in freedom, and to be free means to be rid of any universal law or norm which is external to one's own autonomous personality. The Existential man is the creator of his own law.

Friedrich Nietzsche was born in 1844. His father was a minister in Rocken, Germany. He studied classic literature at Bonn and Leipzig and at the age of twenty-five was appointed to the Chair of literature at the University of Basel. After ten years, poor health forced him to give up his position. He devoted the next thirty years to writing, until in 1889 he was seized by an incurable mental disease, and died in 1900.

The life of Nietzsche, as that of Kierkegaard, was one of tragedy. His own manner of life was in flagrant conflict with the deepest tendency of his view of life. In the latter, Nietzsche constantly praised the *Uebermensch*, the

10

tyrant, who with inexhaustible strength sought to push life forward to new and higher achievements. The tragedy of his life was also heightened by an inner contradiction in his own soul between the Dionysian and the Apollonian man; the former sought to enjoy life in an unrestrained manner and the latter sought to contemplate it with restrained philosophic calm. The will of Nietzsche warred against his intellect until he finally succumbed under the strain.

The philosophy of Nietzsche is divided into three periods. During the first he was under the influence of Schopenhauer's pessimistic philosophy of the will. At this time Nietzsche concluded that the will could be redeemed from its restlessness by art. But even in this early period he spoke of the ideal of a future race which would be nobler and which would exercise a stronger will in order to reach unknown heights. This new culture-man will no longer allow himself to be bound by tradition and authority, and his esthetic freedom will know no restrictions.

The intellectual Appollinian outlook toward life dominated Nietzsche's second period during which he sought the highest end of life in science. Science became the expression of the free spirit and the bearer of culture. Science knows no limits or higher authority; it is completely unrestrained. Its task is to liberate the real concrete man and to make him the master of his own fate. Science liberates man from that which is beyond the sensory. It is not metaphysics or a theory concerning a reality which lies beyond that which can be concretely experienced. Real science is based upon the facts alone; it is positive science. The scientific outlook did not hold Nietzsche permanently but was violently replaced by the Dionysian passion, the desire to realize one's personality in *a lust for power*. Thus Nietzsche arrived at his thesis

11

that the strongest motive in man is the *will to power*. Every human action ought to be subordinated to this basic drive. The will to power ought to be experienced to the fullest degree; it ought not to be restrained or inhibited. The ideal of power is beyond pragmatic norms of good and evil, and has nothing to do with them. That which is really good is that which is born of power. What is good gratifies and increases the lust for power. And what is evil proceeds from weakness and diminishes power and might.

Nietzsche also applied this transvaluation of values to the field of knowledge. His expression "nothing is true, everything is permitted," means that we are no longer concerned with the truth of a statement. A proposition is of interest only insofar as it serves to advance our life and increase our power.

The average, everyday man, the bourgeois, is a mass man, a member of the herd. In contrast to the mass man, Nietzsche posited the ideal of the *"Ubermensch,"* the superman—the tyrant. The superman will create a new culture and a new morality. In this new life he will rule over the herd with astonishing power. The current morality of the herd is the Christian slave morality. The new morality is that of the *Masters (Herrenmoral)*; it is diametrically opposed to slave morality. According to the new morality the superman, the tyrant, has the right and the duty to trample underfoot anything that gets in his way. He must develop the vital energy of man and defend the will to power against anything which resembles humility, sympathy, or any other Christian virtue. Concepts such as piety, redemption, sin, and grace belong to the dispossessed slave morality. *Herrenmoral* is openly anti-Christian.

At times Nietzsche characterizes the superman as a genius or exceptional personality who imposes his own will upon the masses. On other occasions, however, he speaks of the superman as a type of a higher and stronger race which will subsequently inhabit the earth. In any case, this ideal of personality is decidedly individualistic in character, and the superman is free from all law. He lives in absolute freedom and arbitrariness. In place of faith in God and in the immortality of the soul Nietzsche substituted a faith in the eternal reoccurrence of all things. History will infinitely repeat itself in the same form.

Many of Nietzsche's motives have been productive in later Existentialism.

IV

THE NON-PHILOSOPHIC BACKGROUND OF EXISTENTIALISM

A PHILOSOPHER exerts an influence because of his ability and intellectual powers, and of course the person who becomes a philosopher is influenced by his predecessors. He may agree with them or he may radically deviate from past philosophic trends, but he cannot help but be influenced by them. In addition to his philosophical background, a philosopher is also influenced by the circumstances in which he lives. He cannot escape his origin and cultural milieu, and these non-philosophical factors play an integrating role in the formation of a philosophic personality.

That which is true of a philosopher is also true of a philosophical school. We cannot explain the fact that a new school of thought becomes an historical actuality simply because it contains new ideas. New ideas are not enough to explain the power of a certain movement to win adherents and exert an influence; the soil must be fertile in order to nourish new ideas. The cultural situation must be such that in a philosophic guise certain hidden motives find a response in the masses so that they are accepted and propagated by many as the gospel. If one or more philosophers develop a certain philosophy for which the cultural situation is not suitable, then it will not take hold immediately and develop into an influential school. Such philosophers remain solitary figures who are not understood by their time. When the opposite occurs and the conception of a philosopher is accepted by his contemporaries, then we say of such a figure that he understood the deepest motives of his time. Such a phi-

14

losopher is sometimes spoken of as being in advance of his time, as he leaves his impression upon the period of culture which follows him.

As forerunners of Existentialism, Kierkegaard and Nietzsche were in advance of their time; their influence was much greater after their death than during their lifetime. Kierkegaard did not have any great influence prior to the first world war, and Nietzsche did not have a following during his lifetime. Only in the last thirty years has Europe provided fertile ground for the seeds of irrationalism from which contemporary Existentialism has grown.

A few typical characteristics of the cultural situation of the first half of the twentieth century ought to be mentioned.

Preceding centuries were characterized by a cultural optimism. It was thought that in science and technique human reason could rule the world and solve its problems. The future promised progress and prosperity. However, various factors have radically abolished this optimism in the last decades. The enlightened culture has ended in wars and crises, the scope and horror of which were previously unknown. Human science and technique have led to misery and destruction. Science reached depths of human life and existence which it cannot penetrate. Problems have arisen which seem to transcend the power of the human mind, and in Communism and National Socialism tendencies have been brought to light which make absurd the notion of the rationality and intrinsic goodness of human nature. Humanist culture has miserably failed and has given loud voice to its failure; progress has ended in defeat. Modern man has lost any concept of certainty and no longer has a feeling of safety and stability. New calamities, disasters, and catastrophes threaten humanity. Anxiety fills the heart of modern man.

His life is marked by futility, nullity, and the threat of death.

In addition, Christianity is slowly but surely losing its influence on modern man (and this is the deepest religious source of all misery). Old truths which for centuries were never doubted are now cast aside. God, virtue, and immortality are no longer believed in by the masses. Instead, they are denied and opposed with an ever increasing vehemency.

The tendencies which we have enumerated have led to an attitude of decline, *"die Untergang des Abendlandes."* Modern man no longer believes in science. It had promised much and given him little. The humanistic ideal of science has failed and proved to be a sterile phantom. Humanistic thought contains within its basic religious motive a polar tension between nature and freedom.[1] Consequently, when the ideal of science fails, humanistic thought can only seek its salvation in the ideal of personality. Existentialism represents a withdrawal to the irrationalistic structure of the autonomous human personality. Existentialists begin with the concrete human Existence. They do not base their philosophy upon an abstraction of personality such as reason, pure consciousness, "spirit," or something similar. Existentialism is based upon the full human person in his concrete *Existence.* It is based upon the concrete individual with his anxiety, futility, and despair, but also with his resolute determination to account for his hopeless situation and to seek a final stronghold from which he can *existentially experience* and accept his own concrete Existence. Existentialism is in the first place anthropology; some of its representatives may try to arrive at an ontology, a theory of being other than man, but even their primary interest is anthropology.

[1] Cf. Dooyeweerd, *Op. cit.* Vol. I.

There are many characteristics which the various systems of Existentialism have in common, but in spite of this common nucleus and starting point, the various systems differ radically in their detailed construction and are often diametrically opposed to each other on cardinal points. This is not surprising when we consider that both positive Christians and convinced atheists seek to find in Existentialism a philosophic foundation for their outlook toward life and the world. We are now ready to examine individual existentialist philosophers.

Chapter II

EXISTENTIALISM PROPER

I

JASPERS

Karl Jaspers was born in 1883. He was a professor at the University of Heidelberg until his dismissal by the Nazi regime in 1937. After the war he resumed his former duties at Heidelberg until he accepted a position at the University of Basel. He is famous for his *Psychology of World-Views* in which he tried to characterize all possible views of the world. As a philosopher he is influenced by Kierkegaard. His Existentialism occupies an intermediary position between atheistic nihilism and Christianity. He believes in the "transcendent," a philosophical god, which is the object of philosophic faith, but does not reveal himself. He is a negative god who is hidden and maintains an eternal silence. We can know nothing of him but can only believe in him. Because we are absolutely free we are completely independent of this god. If the latter were to exercise any influence upon the life of the real existential men, he would detract from man's autonomy. Thus Jaspers wishes to base the humanistic ideal of personality upon a *voluntaristic individualistic subjectivism.*[1]

Now, the main question asked by all existentialists is,

[1] Tr. note. The meaning of this terminology will become clear in the course of the discussion. D.H.F.

"What is being?" When asked by existentialists, this question has a different meaning than when it is raised in Thomistic metaphysics. Existentialists do not desire to construct an abstract and universal concept of being; they only wish to raise the question, "In what concrete way is it meaningful to speak of being-in-the-world?"

Jaspers answers that being-as-such, being-in-general, is not to be defined. In our concrete life we are only confronted with three specific *forms* of being. First, there is the *being-in-itself-of-things (an-sich-sein)*, whose existence we can conceive of apart from our own Existence. Secondly, there is the *being-object (Gegenstand-sein)* of things, when they are related to a person as subject. Things exist as objects when they are related to me as a subject. The third form of being we only encounter in man, *in being-I, (ich-sein)*. *Being-I* includes being and being known. Only man is and knows that he is. In man being is a being-for-itself *(für-sich-sein)*. None of these three forms of being have any primacy with respect to each other; all three are always present simultaneously. My *Dasein,* my *being-there,* is distinguished from the other forms of being by the fact that I am a *thinking being,* I have consciousness. Thus, to analyze human *Dasein or being-I* we must analyze our consciousness which is characterized in a twofold manner. It is *intentional* and *reflexive.* The intentional character of consciousness means that it is always directed toward objects. These objects do not have to be things, they can also be other persons. The reflexive character of consciousness means that consciousness is not only directed toward objects other than itself. Thought can also turn into itself. I am conscious of my own consciousness. Reflexive consciousness is self-consciousness. Both aspects of consciousness, consciousness of objects and consciousness of the self, can never be separated from each other. They always go together. *Intentional* thought is always accompanied by self consciousness. When I think of objects I know that it is I who thinks about something other than myself.

Science is not able to comprehend the depths of my consciousness. Psychology, logic, and a scientific anthropology are powerless in this respect. They encounter insurmountable barriers behind which lies the deepest foundation of my consciousness, the so-called *existential consciousness*. Philosophy alone can furnish light. But philosophy is not a science, and there is no gradual transition from science to philosophy; the gap is only bridged by the few who are willing to take the leap. The veritable existential outlook toward life is only attained by a few. And this statement reveals the aristocratic tendency of Jasper's thought.

Philosophy can only penetrate to the depths of human existential consciousness by means of *"Existenz-erhellung,"* the enlightenment or illumination of my Existence. The central question in Existentialism is, "What is meant by the concept of *Existence?"* Although formulated differently, there is an essential agreement among existentialists concerning the answer to this question. Existence may never be equated with our mere concrete existence as perceived by the senses. Nor is it merely human consciousness as evidenced in intentional and reflexive thought. Existence is not a perceivable or definable being. It is not an *actualized* being but a *potential*-being. My Existence is my *being-together-with-all-its-possibilities.* As an existential person I am the origin of myself, the creator of the actualization of my potentialities. In my existential being I *transcend* myself, I go beyond my *factual-being,* my being in the present, and I project myself into the future. To exist is to transcend oneself and to constitute oneself. At the moment, I am not completed Existence, but, I am on the way to becoming *Existence.* A prerequi-

20

site to my becoming *Existence* is that I am absolute freedom in my Existence. I choose myself, I elect my possibilities, and decide what I am and what I shall become. To characterize this form of Existence S. U. Zuidema uses the expression "*man as history*," that is to say, human Existence does not only unfold itself in its temporal aspects in an historical development. Man does not merely transcend the temporal aspects in his soul, his deepest religious concentration point.[1] Much more than this is meant by existentialists. The *total* man is *resolved* in history. Man is history. He is permanent *self-unfolding and self-actualization*. Actually I can never say: 'I am,' for at the same moment that I give utterance to this expression I am no longer the same; I am different than I was at the preceding moment. I have transcended or gone beyond what I was. I continually transcend myself. My entire history is historical. My future is possibility; my present is choice, decision; and my past is fixation. In existential action, action in unconditional freedom, eternity appears in time.

From all that has been said it follows that Existence can never be perceived. We can never observe the Existence of another; it can only be discovered in myself. It can only be experienced as my own Existence, in communication with other Existence. However, true communication between two persons in their existential being is never a permanent communion. It is only an incidental contact in rare moments, during which time the deepest ground of being of another is open to my Existence. Such real communication is the highest form of social inter-

---

[1] Tr. note. The author distinguishes fourteen aspects of reality. The historical aspect is one aspect. Man, according to Spier, transcends the cosmic aspects by his heart or soul. For a detailed presentation of this view see, H. Dooyeweerd, *A New Critique of Theoretical Thought*, and also see Spier's own splendid, *Introduction to Christian Philosophy*, Presbyterian and Reformed Publishing Co. 1953.

course. It is philosophic in character, and in this highest form of personal contact an individual allows his *self* to be discovered by another.

We are now in a position to understand the distinction that Jaspers makes between philosophy and science. Philosophy is a search which proceeds from the center of our Existence, arising from the depths of an individual's personal Existence and seeking to discover its being and meaning. It seeks to discover Existence. Science, in contrast, proceeds from our consciousness. It is always directed toward objects. Real existential being is always a closed book for science. Science is concerned with universally valid knowledge that can be expressed in a system. Philosophy does not strive after this end; its goal is merely to seek clarity concerning itself. It wishes to seek certainty about itself as Existence, and Existence can never be made the object of scientific investigation. The certainty which philosophy desires about itself as possible Existence is not an objective certainty. Jaspers calls it *consciousness of being* or absolute being. Philosophy is not a science; it is a view of life *(Weltanschauung).*

Philosophy cannot reach Existence in a direct way but must seek to expose it indirectly, and this is possible for philosophy since Existence is never isolated in itself. Existence actualizes itself in the world;. it is open for communication with the Existence of another, and, in transcendence, Existence is related to the *transcendent,* the silent and hidden deity. Thus philosophy has a threefold task, namely world-orientation, Existenz-erhellung (illumination of existence), and metaphysics. World-orientation is the never completed knowledge of objects which are in the world; it is partly scientific and partly philosophical. As science it is exclusively concerned with what is objective and universal, and as philosophy it is based upon the results of the positive sciences but does not stop there. It raises deeper questions concerning the being of the world. Such questions are unanswerable to science. For example, philosophy wishes to know: Is the world a whole?, or: Is all being resolved in *objective-being (Gegenstand-sein)?*, or: What is the difference between objective being and subjective being? Philosophical world-orientation makes it plain that science cannot speak the last word. It further makes it evident that the being of the freedom of Existence transcends the objective being-of-things-in-the-world. It goes beyond science and makes it possible for one to reflect upon or turn back to one's true self.

Existenz-erhellung must be sharply distinguished from the analysis of human *Dasein* as consciousness. For such an analysis reveals a structure of consciousness which is universally valid. *Existenz-erhellung,* in contrast, is only concerned with the Existence of one person. It illuminates the existential possibilities of one individual. It gives existential certainty that Existence is free, unconditional, and infinite. It confronts Existence with the countenance of the transcendent. This is the deepest and most decisive manner in which man can be himself, for to stand before the transcendent means to exist as an absolutely sovereign individual.

Such a decisive way of being oneself is found in what Jaspers calls the *Grens situatie* (border situation). *Border-situations* are situations which are unavoidable and inescapable in human life. Suffering, death, guilt, and conflict are such border-situations. The situation that I am always in a specific situation, the fact that all reality is historical-being, and the fact that human *Dasein* is problematical are all border-situations. In all such situations I ask myself questions in Existential *Angst (anxiety)*. These questions are determinative for my existential being. And, while I see myself placed before the transcendent deity, they reveal to me the possibilities of my Existence. At this point "Existenz-erhellung" passes over into metaphysics.

Jaspers' existential philosophy or philosophical religion terminates in metaphysics. Metaphysics is concerned with the search for the transcendent, the search for god. In the border-situations I ask myself questions of my Existence. Can these questions be answered? Yes! But they are not answered in the sense that the transcendent reveals himself to all men alike; it does not reveal certain things for man to believe. Official Christianity is to be radically rejected. It is an *unauthentic* manner of existing, in which autonomous man abandons his absolute freedom and is untrue to himself. To discard one's freedom is unworthy of a man; it is apostasy from one's own Existence. When man misuses his freedom against himself, as in the Christian faith, then he falls into self-betrayal.

Strictly speaking the transcendent does not reveal itself. It is wrapped in eternal silence. Existence asks questions in its search for being, and even though the transcendent is silent these questions are answered. The answer, however, is not a universally valid answer, but it is an answer in symbols, in images, in what Jaspers calls *Chiffre*. The answer that we receive to our questions depends upon the meaning we attach to this symbol, upon the way in which we understand the Chiffre. Thus earthly objects can be signs of the transcendent.

Philosophy terminates in an existential faith. It confronts us with the transcendent, the silent deity who speaks only in symbols. This philosophical faith must ever be renewed, and it constantly confronts us with a decision. Thus the *authentic* attitude toward life is the philosophical. And the distinguishing mark of authentic Existence, of the philosophic attitude, is transcendence, in which our freedom is expressed. What must we transcend in authentic Existence? In the first place, we must transcend the world in its objectivity, the world with which science is so concerned. The common man, the mass man, is resolved in his unauthentic Existence in this objective world. But the existential *Angst* in the Grenssituations frees *Existence* from this objective unauthentic Existence. As a result, we lose all "objective" certainty and gain instead an existential certainty which enables us to face anxiety with bravery and courage. We are thrown back upon ourselves. We are thrown into despair, but we retain faith in ourselves, and in our own freedom and responsibility to ourselves. We have the faith that we are a law unto ourselves and are free to actualize our own potentialities. Therefore, in his authentic Existence *Man* transcends himself. He transcends his concrete historical Existence which exists here and now and is, so to speak, on the way to becoming his authentic self. He is ever busy to become himself. He arrives at himself. This takes place in communication with others because philosophic communication can arouse transcendence in others. Nevertheless, authentic Existence remains essentially enclosed in solitude. And finally, in true philosophy the existential man transcends his own Existence in the experience of the deity. The experience of the transcendent is the highest self realization of the free autonomous man.

In the beginning of this section we characterized the conception of Karl Jaspers as voluntaristic, individualistic, and subjectivistic. The meaning of this terminology can now be understood. Radical subjectivism seeks the law for life in the subject. It is evident that Jaspers is a subjectivist in this sense, as he holds that autonomous man, in his authentic Existence, is the creator of his own law. If a person submits to a law which he did not himself create, he abandons his freedom and falls from authentic Existence.

Jaspers is also an individualist. In authentic Existence

man exists in solitude. It is true that he is confronted by the transcendent, but he does not have any real communication with the deity. And even in philosophic communication with others he is always thrown back upon himself.

Voluntarism is also unmistakeable in Jaspers' thought. The essence of man is not reason; it is not thought, but the absolute freedom of the will. Analytical thought is all right for science, as the latter is concerned with the objective being of the world. But this objective being is of a lower order than existential being. Existential being is in a constant state of transcendence. It seeks after transcendent being and seeks to actualize the ideal of personality.

The philosophy of Jaspers is further characterized by pessimism. The highest goal that man can reach in authentic Existence is faith in oneself in the midst of *despair*. This faith-in-oneself is born out of and accompanied by *Angst*. The final end reached by this philosophical religion is that the existential man experiences true being in his own failure to be infinite.

II

MARTIN HEIDEGGER

Martin Heidegger was born in 1889. He was strongly influenced by the phenomenology of Husserl, according to whom phenomenology is the basic science for philosophy; philosophy becomes a science through phenomenology. The latter does not investigate being but seeks the meaning and significance of things. It seeks their *"essence."* These *essences* are found in the field of the so-called pure, absolute, or transcendental consciousness. In its method phenomenology seeks to inspect essences. This inspection of essences can only be applied after a "transcendental reduction" has taken place. In this reduction a thing is abstracted from its concrete individual existence and the essences of phenomena are contemplated in pure consciousness, and are then inspected and described.

Heidegger succeeded Husserl as professor of philosophy at the University of Freiburg in 1928. He remained faithful to the method of phenomenology. His most important work, in which he developed his existentialist views, was published in 1927 under the title *"Sein und Zeit"* (1927). Heidegger was known only to his colleagues, until his international reputation was developed by the writings of his former student, Sartre.

What is the content of Heidegger's Existentialism? He intends to arrive finally at a general ontology, a universal theory of being. He believes philosophy can no longer limit itself to epistemology, logic, ethics, and esthetics. In Heidegger the old metaphysics lives again in modern ontology, and this fact is connected with the trend in Humanistic thought from rationalism to irrationalism.

27

Although it is Heidegger's intention to develop a general ontology, he has not yet done so. A universal ontology must be preceded by an *"existential analysis of the Dasein,"* that is, an existential theory of human Existence. Such a theory is the subject of *Sein und Zeit.*

The main distinction in *being* is that between the *Dasein ("human being there")* and that which does not belong to the *Dasein.*

The *Dasein (human being there)* is characterized by *Existence. Existence* is significant to the individual in an absolute way. To exist is to exceed oneself; it is to stand outside of oneself and to transcend oneself. It is self-transcendence, never being but always becoming. *[Man as history* (Zuidema)].

Dasein, or *Existence,* is not the total man in the all-sidedness of his existence. It is not all the temporal aspects of man but only an abstraction of the latter. The natural aspects of number, space, motion and life do not belong to *Existence* or *Dasein.* Dasein is composed of a complex of post- or super-*biotic* temporal aspects. And the latter, according to Heidegger, are not religiously concentrated in a super-temporal heart.[1] *Existence* rests in itself and is not based upon the natural aspects; nevertheless, the latter are not disconnected from the *Dasein* but are correlative to it. The natural aspects are in themselves mean-

---

[1] Tr. note. The author is a member of a school of philosophy which has been developed systematically particularly by Hermann Dooyeweerd. According to this view the aspects of reality are arranged in an architectonic cosmic law order. The natural aspects are those of number, space, motion, life, and the psychical sphere. The post-biotic aspects are the aspects which follow the biotic aspect. They include the psychical, analytical, historical, linguistical, social, economic, esthetic, juridical, ethical spheres and the sphere of faith. This order is not arbitrary as the higher aspects follow the lower. However, in reality all aspects exist in an unbreakable coherence and are only distinguished and analyzed by scientific thought. Man concentrates all these aspects in his heart, the religious centrum of his existence. *(A New Critique of Theoretical Thought)* D.H.F.

ingless. They depend upon Existence as it alone can give them meaning.

How do we learn to know the *Dasein?* We cannot learn to know it by objective thought, since it can never be an object for the knowing subject. Since it is pure *subjectivity,* the meaning of the *Dasein* is hidden to objective thinking. The *Dasein* reveals itself only to itself; as such, it is super-rational or pre-rational. We can only learn what the *Dasein* is from a revelation from the *Dasein.* And this revelation from the *Dasein* to itself is only understood in a phenomenological analysis. The philosophy which furnishes such an analysis is not a science but is of a super-scientific character. In science our minds operate with general concepts or categories, but in philosophy we employ ontological distinctions or *"existentialia."*

Heidegger also makes an important distinction between *authentic* and *unauthentic Dasein.* He distinguishes between Existence which really exists and Existence which has fallen away from true Existence (*Verfallensein*). Unauthentic Existence is the general attitude toward life of the large masses of people. The masses flee from their own responsibility and voluntarily abandon their own freedom. They are resolved or absorbed in the world. Philosophy must depart from this unauthentic Existence and unmask its deception. Only in this way can it arrive at the *mode of being* of the authentic *Dasein.*

Unauthentic *Dasein* is preoccupied with the *externals* of humanity. It loses itself in society and the masses (*Das Man*). It listens to an hypostatized *Mankind,* the One like the many, *the Man.* The average, common, everyday man does not act independently and freely. He acts as *Man* acts. He behaves as *One* does (*Das Man*) and avoids doing anything that is not done by everyone else. The mass-man is no longer himself; he does not dare to live. Public opinion is his norm. A person who is lost in the

One does not reflect on authentic Existence or being. He is driven about with each passing tide and is tossed upon the waves of society and the world. He runs away from himself. He is *fallen* from his true self and no longer understands what real *Dasein* is. His sole activity is *Care* (*Sorge*). He is occupied with the many things which are in the world and with the countless people that surround him.

All human *Existence* or *Dasein* is, in essence, Existence. That is to say, it is *self-determination, self-projection,* or *self-transcendence.* Existence is to have the potentiality of Being (Seinkonnen). Man is his potentialities; he constantly chooses one of his potentialities and thus projects and actualizes himself in the future. The *Dasein* is never identical with itself. *Dasein* is not static. It is always something different than it was. It is always becoming itself, and in becoming himself man is a law unto himself, the creator of his own norm. For all *Dasein* is characterized by *freedom.* Dasein can misuse its freedom by choosing against itself. As a result, man loses himself and his autonomy; his free self-determination changes into heteronomy. As he now bows before norms which are foreign to him, norms which he did not make, his Existence perishes in the world of *daily life.*

Authentic Existence must be sharply distinguished from unauthentic Existence, yet both are forms of *Dasein.* They are antithetical forms of *Dasein,* but they cannot be separated from each other. Authentic Existence is only a modus, a manner of being, of unauthentic Existence, and the latter always has priority.

One of the Existentialia of *Dasein* is that *Dasein* is always *being-in-the-world (sein-in-der-Welt).* But what is the world? The world is not a given or datum.[1] The

[1] Tr. note. The world is not the empirical world. It is not the totality of natural things open to scientific investigation. D.H.F.

world is not separate from our Existence. It is not a field in which the *Dasein* can project and transcend itself. No, the world first arises by reason of the self transcending of the *Dasein*. It is the projection of all the possibilities of the *Dasein*, and not the totality of objects which we use and concern ourselves with, for the world precedes every object. The *Dasein* and man is always busy in this world with the task (*Sorgen*) of incorporating the objects and things into the world of the *Dasein*. This incorporation of things into the world is called *"objectization."*

What is the meaning of all things which are in the world? They have only a pragmatic meaning; they are utensils. Things do not exist because of their own initiative and will, but in order to be employed by man. If we reflect about a utensil (*das Zuhandene*), it becomes an object, but the objectivity of a thing does not exhaust its meaning. Its meaning is not *to be reflected upon* but *to be used* and employed. Things are incorporated into the world of the *Dasein* by being used. Thus Existence is a *being-concerned-in-the-world* (*sorgend-in-der-Welt-sein*). It is to occupy and to use things which are in the world.

To the unauthentic human Existence, the world is only environment, the totality of all objects. The real world, the world of the authentic Existence, is broader than the environment. It is more than all the objects. It is the transcendence, the projection produced in the process by which the *Dasein* constitutes itself. The real world is foreign to the unauthentic Existence of the everyday man. The mass man is *resolved* in objects, in the pragmatic *Care* (*Sorgen*). To attain authentic Existence a person must no longer view himself as one of the many objects of his environment. He must transcend pragmatism, the attitude of unauthentic Existence. Pragmatism is exclusively concerned with the utility of things. It is concerned with what can advance and sustain our life; even science belongs to unauthentic Existence.

Being-together, mit-sein, existing together with other beings of the kind of *Dasein,* is also one of the *existentialia* of *Dasein.* In this *mit-sein, Dasein* constitutes the *public* world. Unauthentic Existence also degrades this public world to environment, to the One, to which man subjects himself in his apostate Existence. But authentic Existence experiences this relation to others in full freedom and responsibility as one of Care (Sorge).

The One, Das Man, is also one of the existentialia of Dasein and therefore belongs to the structure of human Existence. As one of the existentialia it is an original and intrinsic characteristic of Existence. Unauthentic Existence places its responsibility, freedom, and self-transcendence upon the shoulders of *Das Man* of culture. And thus this fallen Existence ends in slavery. As a result unauthentic man enjoys rest. He is certain and feels at home in his environment.

The basic structure of human Existence is the *mood of Care*[1] *(Stimmung der Sorge).* This Care expresses itself in three things: first, in the discovery that human Existence is a *thrown* Existence *(Geworfen-sein).* Man has not called himself into being. He cannot help it that he is there, but must accept the fact as something that has occurred outside of his will. Secondly, Care expresses itself in *understanding (Verstehen).* By this is meant self-projection, self-transcendence which signifies that everyday life makes use of the possibilities which lie in the future, so that we unceasingly transcend ourselves. And in the third place, Care expresses itself in the result of this self-projection. It expresses itself in the fact that in this way *Dasein* establishes a world and a community. By ordering and systematizing *Dasein* produces a cosmos and a society.

[1] Tr. note. *Care is the Being of Dasein.* D.H.F.

Now, the cardinal question in the philosophy of Heidegger is, "How can man pass over from unauthentic Existence, which is primary, to the mode of being of authentic Existence?" The answer is that man is saved from unauthentic Existence by *Angst*. *Angst* must be sharply distinguished from fear. Fear is always the fear of something; it is brought about by an object. *Angst* in contrast is unspecified. It arises suddenly out of the depths of our Existence and surprises us without any apparent reason.

Angst is a powerful means of revelation which can bring about a great change in human Existence, for it confronts the latter with itself. Man discovers himself in *Angst*. In it he withdraws in solitude from the world of his environment and society. *Angst* reveals the world and existential Existence to us. It also makes us no longer at home in the world (*Unheimlichkeit*). It makes man lonely and causes him to experience his Existence in its totality—in its limitation due to the fact that it cannot escape death.

Unauthentic Existence flees from this totality and will not learn of it. It lives as though it were endless. Unauthentic Existence loses itself in the world and in *Das Man*. It is, therefore, not concerned with death. When *Angst* enters our life, the delusion of unauthentic Existence is broken through, and authentic Existence discovers itself in a threefold manner.

Angst reveals, in the first place, the *thrown-ness* (*geworfenheit*) of Existence, the factuality of our existential Existence which is not self caused. We cannot help it that we are there. In the second place, our freedom to choose and produce our own possibilities is revealed to us in *Angst*. And finally, in *Angst* we learn that Existence is *being-toward-death (Sein-zum-Tode)*, Existence is permeated with death and determined by it.

Our *conscience* is awakened by this *Angst;* it claims

attention for itself. The conscience is human Existence in its state of *no-longer-being-at-ease, no-longer-feeling-at-home-in-the-world.* Our conscience calls us out of the apostasy of unauthentic Existence and causes us to return to authentic Existence by making us choose and actualize our own possibilities. Whenever the conscience is aroused a *feeling of guilt* (Schuldig-sein) is also awakened. This feeling of guilt does not have anything to do with sin in the Christian sense. To feel guilty, according to Heidegger, is to take upon oneself the burden of having been thrown into Existence. It is the voluntary acceptance of the destiny that human Existence factually exists. This means that man in his authentic Existence feels guilty because he is not self-sufficient and completely equal with God. He feels guilty because the words of Satan, "Ye shall be as God," cannot be fully realized!

However, when man accepts his own *geworfenheit,* the fact that he is thrown into existence, then man becomes the ground of his own nullity (*Nichtigkeit*). Thus, the humanistic theory of freedom here turns into a pessimistic doctrine of nullity. And the ideal of personality is undermined by nihilism.

Nullity also exists in human Existence in a three-fold manner: there is first the nullity of Existence which arises because man is a *thrown-existence (Geworfen-sein)* and is therefore guilty. It is not only man's guilt that he did not create himself, but this fact is also a proof of his nullity (*Nichtigkeit*). Secondly, human Existence is nullity (*Nichtig*) because it is finite in the future (it ends in death). It is an Existence-toward-death. It is lived between the limits of perishability. This second form of *nullity* is not characterized as guilt. And finally there is the nullity due to the fact that in his continual self transcendence man can only choose and realize one of many possibilities. He can never realize all possibilities at the same time. What is our crowning achievement, namely, self-projection and self-transcendence, is at the same time our poverty, our privation, our nullity.

Human Existence in its past, present and future is saturated and permeated with nullity. Nevertheless, it does not entirely sink away into *nothing (das Nichts)*. But it still retains a little positive meaning because *Existence* remains a finite freedom and is the performance and actualization of a positive choice. But in all this Existence is a *freedom-toward-death (Freiheit-zum-Tode)*. In his unauthentic Existence man does not know and accept this and is therefore unconsciously given over to the meaninglessness of life.

Authentic being is thus an Existence in freedom-toward-death *(Freiheit-zum-Tode)*. Whoever wishes to experience this authentic being must face death directly and not seek to camouflage the fact that he is going to die. This does not mean that man is comforted with respect to death. But in authentic Existence he accepts it uncomforted, as the most proper possibility of his Existence. Death is not a force which is foreign to our Existence; it is not something which deceptively overtakes us by surprise, but it belongs to our Existence in a very essential way. It arises out of our Existence and terminates it. It is the possibility of the impossibility of Existence. It is the radical finitude and nullity of Existence.

Death is the most proper possibility of Existence. And this implies the absolute subjectivity of *being-toward-death (Dasein)*. For death has nothing to do with the world around us. It is concerned only with human *Dasein*. It deceives us fatally and destroys us finally; therefore, being-toward-death *(Sein-zum-Tode)* is not related to anything else. It withdraws us from our being-concerned-in-the-world *(Sorgend-in-der-Welt-sein)*, and throws us back upon ourselves and encloses us in our own individuality. The certainty of the possibility of death determines its fury and inescapableness. This possibility deceives us permanently. *Sein-zum-Tode* is the certainty of the uncertainty of Existence.

Death can never be overcome. It is never to be replaced by any other possibility. Death and the grave are unavoidable. To think that death can be overcome is an idle illusion. Death dominates all the other possibilities of human Existence. Its shadow falls as a deceptive destiny over the whole of life and marks it as *nullity*.

True wisdom in this disconsolate Existence is to face death in freedom. It is to be ready to meet with a grim determination this possibility which properly belongs to Existence. In true wisdom we accept the fact that we are not at home in the world and accept our Existence in absolute solitude. The authentic man is conscious of the vanity of Existence and freely accepts death. He understands the call of conscience which calls him to accept a nihilistic future. He accepts nothingness and the meaninglessness of life.

Heidegger's pseudo-religious view of life does not end here, but has a remarkable conclusion. The attitude of the everyday man is degraded in Heidegger. He disparages pragmatic Existence which unauthentically uses the world and society for its own advantage. Yet—and this is what is remarkable—after we have seen the meaninglessness of pragmatic Existence, we can return to it and accept it for what it is. Since a person who is authentic knows that he is *free-toward-death,* he possesses an inexhaustible tolerance and endless patience. He can, therefore, return to the world of his environment and take part in the activity of the masses. The only difference is that he has seen through the delusion of life, is certain of the nullity of Existence and bears it as an inalienable possession.

One thing that strikes us immediately is that Heidegger is principally an atheist in his thought. He remains hostilely silent with respect to God. And yet upon close examination we see that his philosophy is negatively orientated toward Christianity. He constantly uses specific Christian terms such as guilt and conscience. Of course, he interprets these terms in a secular way. His entire *religious* system is a part of a modern culture which is bent upon the secularization of Christianity.

It is difficult to characterize Heidegger's Existentialism in a single word. In a certain sense it is still humanistic, for it is an irrationalistic defense of the ideal of personality, and this ideal is one of the basic motives of modern Humanism. On the other hand, its philosophy is a consistent nihilism which accepts a disqualified pragmatism. Its ideas shift between a pragmatic and a nihilistic pole, and undoubtedly the accent falls upon the latter. Heidegger ends in a dark attitude of nullity which cannot be penetrated by the faintest glimmer of hope.

This conception is still a humanistic philosophy of freedom, but its irrationalistic character is displayed in a typical Existentialist manner, which is especially evident in the fact that Heidegger affirms that no one can be redeemed from unauthentic Existence by merely accepting his theory. One cannot attain the freedom and wisdom of authentic Existence by merely believing in Heidegger's doctrine. Authentic Existence is only reached through existential *Angst*. To reach the place where the individual is conscious of his freedom-toward-death a person must personally experience this *Angst* in the very depths of his being. It is possible that a person who has never heard of Heidegger's theory may arrive at authentic Existence, and it is equally possible that another person who knows Heidegger's theory may never attain to the real wisdom of authentic Existence.

CHAPTER III

EXISTENTIALISM IN FRANCE

WE HAVE thus far given a short summary of two German existentialists, Jaspers and Heidegger. We shall now devote our attention to several French existentialists.

Existentialism has found fertile soil in France and displays there a slightly different character than in Germany. H. J. Pos made the following comment on this point: "Even when the form and the content of French Existentialism is modeled after the German, the French brand remains milder and more universally human than the source of its inspiration."[1] And A. de Waelhens wrote on the same question: "The secondary causes of its entry and the traditional differences between German and French thought make it quite understandable that French Existentialism has never reached the same intensity. French thought is traditionally influenced by the idea that philosophy is an explanatory description of our experience in all its richness. Consequently, existential feelings may acquire a privileged but not an all dominating position.[2]

This second nuance of French Existentialism is not only because the French have a different mentality from the Germans, but it is also partly due to the fact that their philosophical background is somewhat different. Like German Existentialism, the French variety is also ori-

[1] In an article entitled *Leon Brunschvicq en zijn betekenis voor de hedendaagse wijsbegeerte* in *Alg. Ned. Tijdschrift voor Wijsbegeerte en Psychologie*, May 1947, p. 115.

[2] *De Franse wijsbegeerte tijdens en sedert de oorlog*, in *Alg. Ned. Tijdschrift voor Wijsbegeerte en Psychologie*, May 1947, p. 121.

entated toward the anti-idealistic ideas of Kierkegaard and the phenomenological method of Husserl. In addition, however, Existentialism in France is especially influenced by the spirit of MAINE DE BIRAN.

Maine de Biran was a remarkable figure (1766-1824). Like Kierkegaard, he was not an academic philosopher and did not hold to the philosophy of his day.[1] It is negatively to De Biran's credit that he sharply combatted the ideology of his day, especially that of Condillac (1715-1780). Condillac based his views upon the thesis that, "no matter what the soul may be, the content of its acts of consciousness only proceed from sensory perception."[2] The totality of all spiritual acts develops out of perception through association. Knowledge and morality grow out of the sensory. This naturalistic philosophy was accompanied by an absolute rejection of all metaphysics. Condillac did not wish to penetrate to the reality of the human spirit or to the reality of a world beyond sensory impressions.

Such a view could only lead to reaction. We must clearly understand, however, that this conflict is carried on solely in humanist and not in Christian philosophy. Humanist philosophy rests upon the religious basic themes of nature and freedom. When humanist thought is dominated by the ideal of science, primacy is ascribed to nature. The attempt is then made to explain all of reality in terms of natural scientific method. The system of Condillac illustrates that when the method of the natural sciences is consistently applied there is no longer room for the free human personality in naturalistic thought. This exclusion of the free personality gives rise to a reac-

[1] Tr. note. See Dooyeweerd, *op. cit.* Vol. I., and A. de Waelhens: *Hoofdtrekken van het Frans existentialism*, in *Ned. Tijdschrift.* Oct. 1947, p. 1 ff.
[2] Windelband-Heimsoeth: *Lehrbuch der Geschichte der Philosophie*, 1935, pp. 383 and 400.

tionary movement based upon the religious idea of freedom and the humanistic ideal of personality. This reaction seeks to reserve a place for the autonomy of human personality.

The ideal of personality vehemently comes to the foreground in the views of De Biran. De Biran placed the accent upon the *einheitliche Aktivität des Bewusztseins*,[1] upon the unity of the spirit or of the ego which arises as a *totality*. His conception is explicitly voluntaristic. In the human will we directly experience our own activity and the opposition of the non-ego. De Biran changed the Cartesian principle, *Cogito ergo sum* (I think, therefore, I am) to *volo ergo sum* (I will, therefore, I am). At the foundation of all the *spiritual* sciences he laid the principle of the self-consciousness of the willing personality.[2] Sensations and their association do not lead to the certainty and directness of the concept of the self. Moreover, the ego is not a thing which becomes conscious of its existence by itself. The ego does not exist in isolation. Self-consciousness arises through the *exertion* which proceeds from the willing ego and which is also arrested by the *resistance* of the non-ego. Exertion and resistance necessarily go together in order to bring about self-consciousness. This opposition of the non-ego, which must be overcome by the exertion of the willing ego, lies especially in the body. This gives rise to another characteristic of this conception, namely, that each act of consciousness rests upon a movement or resistance of the human body.

According to Waelhens[3] the influence of Biranism is responsible for the fact that "the growth—and in any case the triumph—of every radical idealism in France

[1] *Ibid.* p. 537.

[2] *Ibid.* p. 538.

[3] *Hoofdtreekken van het Frans Existentialisme,"* in *Alg. Ned. Tijdschrift voor Wijsbegeerte en Psychologie,* Oct. 1947, p. 2.

has been definitely retarded." Waelhens also writes: "The fact that France trusts in the existential experience is undeniably due to Maine De Biran and to the diffused influence of his spirit and tradition."[1]

The influence of De Biran is concretely seen in the philosophy of Le Senne. The latter had originally been under the influence of the theoretical idealism of the French neo-Kantian Hamelin. However, he departed from this theoretical idealism in favor of a description of concrete consciousness. Rene Le Senne originally followed the dialectical idealism of Hamelin, but he has now rejected this on the basis of the concrete experience of the ego. Le Senne and Louis Lavelle are the forces behind the contemporary movement, *Philosophie de L'Esprit*.

Hamelin had viewed contradictions as a property of dialectical thought. Le Senne, in contrast, contemplates contradiction as a component of human experience. It is the duty of man to conquer contradiction. But this reconciliation does not take place in thought. It occurs "in the invention (sometimes in the discovery) of a conciliatory-fact or -situation."[2] It occurs in a fact that reconciles the contradiction. Such a reconciliation "retains the positive value of the contradictory situations but it abolishes their opposing character in the creating novelty of the reconciliation."[3]

The influence of Biran is evident in the fact that in overcoming contradiction man becomes himself to a greater degree. And in this we uncover one of the basic tendencies of Existentialism, namely, that the authentic being of man is the transcendence of himself, self projection. Le Senne calls his view *idée-existentialisme* (the word *idea* makes us think of his early orientation toward

[1] *Ibid.* p. 3.
[2] *Ibid.* p. 4.
[3] *Ibid.* p. 4.

41

the idealism of Hamelin). He holds that this transcendence of contradiction is accompanied by an increase in self-consciousness.

This ends our preliminary sketch of the background of French Existentialism. We are now ready to examine the views of Marcel, Lavelle and Sartre.

I

MARCEL

BORN in 1889, Gabriel Marcel's early training was free from any religious influence. Prior to his becoming a teacher of philosophy, Marcel studied both philosophy and literature. Especially noteworthy is the fact that his studies brought him closer and closer to Christianity until at the age of forty he was baptised as a member of the Roman Catholic Church. During his philosophical training Marcel was influenced by English Hegelianism and the rationalism of the French philosopher *Brunschvicq*. However, by his own independent thinking he freed himself from the abstract dialectic of his teachers and substituted in its place a phenomenological view of human Existence. He called his own philosophy a *"higher empiricism,"*[1] because he took his starting point in "the concrete existing ego that inhabits a qualitative world."

Marcel is an enemy of all systems because they do violence to the truth and press concrete reality into a pre-conceived mold. His rejection of all system is accompanied by an aversion for abstraction which he considers to be a corruption of reality. Only that which is concrete really exists. Veritable reality is that of human Existence, and human Existence is a *mystery*.

One of the main ideas in Marcel is the contrast which he posits between a *problem* and a *mystery*. A problem is something impersonal. The scientist is busy with problems. He remains objectively distant from his science and his labors are impersonal. Scientific problems and solutions are objective things which do not touch the deepest *being* of the scientist who is totally unmoved by them.

[1] *Ibid.* p. 6.

The scientist is not *engaged* by the problems of science. The result of all science is a dehumanization of reality.

The science of history, for example, informs us of many facts concerning the life of Napoleon. It uses the name "Napoleon" as a short symbolical representation of the entire complex of data and facts which comprised the course of Napoleon's life. But Napoleon himself, the concrete living personality who transcendently stands behind all these facts, is completely lost in this complex of objective data. The science of history does not throw any light upon his Existence. In fact it only obscures the real Existence of Napoleon, and this is only the first *dehumanization.*

The second dehumanization takes place in the person of the scientist. If the scientist were *to engage* himself with the Existence of Napoleon, he would then employ his own intuitive understanding to penetrate into Napoleon's concrete living personality, and in this process the personality of the scientist would itself be increased as he would then transcend the factuality of his own Existence. But this penetration of the person does not occur in science. Science eliminates the person and in its stead substitutes diverse objective data with the result that the person of the scientist is withdrawn from the activity of science. The person of the scientist is unaffected by his science. The problems of science escape and pass by his Existence.[1]

It is clear from the preceding that for Marcel there is a narrow connection between the manner in which we know and the manner in which we exist. If we view another person as an impersonal "*he,*" as an impersonal man, then we ourselves become a "*he,*" a man without authentic Existence. However, we need not continue to be unauthentic Existence. If we transcend the factuality of our

[1] *Op. cit.* p. 7ff.

life we can *really* exist and thus escape the condition of being a "he." And this escape occurs when we speak of another person as a *"thou,"* as an existential man who transcends his own factuality. In this engagement of ourselves with the transcending Existence of another, we ourselves become a "thou," a transcending person.

This existential self-transcendence is limited. Man can never escape his factual determinedness because of his corporality. Consequently, transcendence is a never ending process. It never reaches a perfect state and never becomes a possession. Human transcendence is stimulated, however, by the hope in a perfect *Person* who is detached from all factual determinedness [through love of God.] Human transcendence is stimulated by a *Person* who is an absolute "Thou." The process of transcendence is absolutely completed in Him as He is not bound to any factuality and is not determined by anything. He can in nowise become an object but is absolutely Himself. And only if man anchors his own person in God can he also become absolutely himself.

Now, what we have just said does not lie on the same *niveau* as the *problems*. It is not on the same level with the objective things of science, but it lies on the plain of mystery to which we are related together with our whole personality. Philosophy, according to Marcel, is concerned with such mysteries. It seeks to understand the very depths of the mystery of human Existence.

A mystery is in principle not capable of being solved. Because we are ourselves a mystery in our permanent self transcendence, we cannot understand ourselves and can never exhaustively say of ourselves: *thus am I*. What I am is always hidden. I can say *what I have,* for what I have lies in the sphere of problems, but I cannot say *what I am.*

But if a mystery cannot be solved the question can be

raised, "Is it meaningful to investigate the meaning of a mystery?" Marcel answers this question in the affirmative. For even though a mystery cannot be solved, yet if we concentrate our attention upon it, we are rewarded by a better understanding of its meaning, and by a clearer vision of its significance. By such contemplation a mystery reveals its richness to us.

Marcel compares these natural mysteries with the mysteries of faith. We cannot comprehend the latter, but we can approach their meaning through faith. We have already seen that Marcel employs the concept of self-transcendence. In this he is similar to other philosophers of Existence who also maintain that man transcends his factual determination and projects himself into the future. On this point, however, Marcel is closer to the view of Jaspers than to that of Heidegger. As a matter of fact, Marcel's view of self transcendence differs essentially from that of Heidegger. Self transcendence according to the latter is necessarily related to the world. It is a *being-concerned-in-the-world* in order to incorporate into the world of authentic being, the objects of the environment of unauthentic Existence.

In Marcel, in contrast, the real transcendence of man takes place in relation to God. Our human Existence is essentially nothing other than a relation of myself to the Absolute Thou, the Absolute Transcendent. Not everyone is conscious of this relation. But even if man is unconscious of the fact, he cannot engage in any action apart from this most fundamental relation of himself to God. At their very roots all my actions participate in the acts of God. My volitions, thoughts, and deeds are necessarily related to what God wills, thinks and does. Without this participation in God, human Existence simply would not be.

The essence of man must be understood in terms of

his actions. Especially relevant to his essence are those deeds which properly belong to man as an expression of his essence, namely, love, hope, and faith.

What is love? The meaning of love is that my life is not closed to that of another person but is intimately opened to him. The love that one human being has for another is based upon the love of God. God and I sustain a mutual relationship to each other, and if in this relationship I am open to another and love him—because God is absolute and perfect Love—then in my relationship to my fellowman I shall also love my neighbor. Thus we open our lives to our neighbor and participate in the love of God, Who opens Himself to us. For this reason veritable human Existence is love. I transcend myself in love; I reveal myself in my love for another and in love I am resolved in another. My own life is in this way enriched. By being open sympathetically to God and my neighbor, my love is enriched, and if I were to shut out the other person and close myself to him, then my own process of self transcendence would be hindered and I would be in violence to my own Existence. By opening my life to God, God is no longer a "He" but a "Thou." And on the basis of this existential relationship, the other person, to whom I open myself in love, is also no longer a "he," but is now a "thou." Where existential love is so experienced, hope is also present. There is also a relation to God in my hopes. For real hope is based upon the conviction that if I desire a thing worthy of being valued, there is a perfect Person who desires the same thing. Hope does not exist outside of this relation with God. Outside of this relation there is only despair. To attain hope we must, therefore, relentlessly seek to overcome despair. However, we must not readily suppose that we have escaped despair, for it can appear in camouflaged form. For example, if a person loses himself in innumerable unimportant details of everyday life, he has not escaped and unmasked despair, but has only forgotten and pushed it aside. Love and hope create communal ties, but despair cuts all such connections and isolates the individual. Love and hope are accompanied by and connected with *fidelity*. True communion is only possible on the basis of fidelity. In faithfulness I transcend my factual attitude and momentary situation. If I give my word to perform a certain act at a later date, then I have determined what I shall later be. By giving my word I specify what I shall be even though my inclinations may be different when the time comes for me to keep my word. I transcend myself and project my personality in fidelity.

To display real fidelity toward my fellows I must give myself completely to God Who is the Faithful One. For this reason fidelity can only rest upon faith in God, and this faith is the highest existential relation in which I transcend myself.

Human Existence is ruled by two fundamental principles. In the first place, my Existence is always a determined Existence that is specified by all sorts of factual conditions. I am always in a concrete situation which is determined by factors of heredity, age, character, environment, and profession.

The second foundation of my Existence is that I sustain a relationship to God in each situation. In other words I share in His life through participation.

From these two basic facts it follows that the essence of my life is that I am related to God. I am in a concrete situation, but I am related to God and participate in Him; I am united to God in my love, hopes, and faithfulness, and in each concrete situation I transcend myself through love, hope, and fidelity. By this participation in God my person is continually formed in permanent self projection.

48

Man is also history in this system of existential philosophy.

Another question which Marcel answers is: "What is the world?" For Marcel the world is not the world of things but of persons; his conception is definitely *personalistic*. Things are always for the use of persons. When things hinder our contract with others their service is negative. Their positive meaning is to advance our relations with our fellows.

One person should be related to another in such a way that he is ever at the command of the other. I must always be ready to answer the call of my fellow man. In fact I do not belong to myself but to others. I am at their disposal and must remain ever willing to respond to their commands. If my possessions interfere with my contact with others, I must detach myself from my possessions and be able to give myself to others in love. Love is correlative to poverty. Everything which bears the slightest likeness to egoism is treason, a betrayal of the love and fidelity which I owe others. It is a betrayal because I release myself in self love from the obligation I have to serve my neighbor. The worse form of unfaithfulness is suicide. And faithfulness reaches its zenith in martyrdom, in which the self is completely denied and sacrificed in the service of others.

Marcel also discusses death, but in a different way than Heidegger. Marcel seeks to remain in a Christian atmosphere, and, unlike Heidegger, is not a fatalist or a nihilist. Heidegger wishes to face death squarely with the courage of despair. His view is in principle without any hope. Marcel, in contrast, views death as the perfection of human life. Life continues after death and the grave. Life exceeds our Existence in the world, which is actually only a preparation for the life which is to come. At death all that we *have* is detached from us, but our

Existence, our being, continues after death.

Marcel also distinguishes between authentic and un-authentic Existence, and there is also a trace of pessimism and tragedy in his conception.

Authentic Existence is a life of love, hope and fidelity, but it is not attained in concrete Existence without a struggle and tension. Love easily falls prey to egoism; hope is readily devoured by despair, and fidelity is permanently deceived by betrayal. This conflict must be accepted and carried on in freedom. Proceeding out of the concrete situation, our personality is formed in autonomous self determination, and we can thus approach the existential mystery of life.

Typical of this Roman Catholic thinker is the fact that he denies any connection between philosophy and Divine Revelation and will not allow his thought to be directed by the Bible, but wishes to base it upon a concrete phenomenological view of the phenomena of experience. For Marcel philosophy belongs to the sphere of nature and does not presuppose any supernatural revelation. At the utmost philosophy can only be the preliminary step to faith in revelation.

In summary we can say that the conception of Marcel —as that of Jaspers—is irrationalistic and subjectivistic in character. The irrationalism of Marcel's view is of a personalistic type and is clearly evident in his depreciation of science in favor of philosophy. Science is only concerned with problems, but philosophy seeks the meaning of mystery, and this meaning is discovered in a super-scientific manner in the Existence of the person. It is discovered by philosophy.

Marcel's view is subjectivistic because of the fact that the autonomous human person freely establishes his own law and exists in free self determination.

And in spite of the emphasis upon the mutual tie between different people, Marcel's view is individualistic because of the emphasis placed upon the Existence of the individual. Communion between different people is constituted by the Existence of separate persons.

II

LAVELLE

ONE of the benefits of the last war is that now scientific interests in Holland have become much broader and are not as exclusively orientated toward Germany. This is also a gain for philosophy as we are now much more willing to pay attention to philosophical movements in other countries. This broadened outlook accounts for our interest in French philosophical thought. It is often thought, although erroneously, that Sartre is the greatest typical figure of contemporary French philosophy. French thought is also represented by Marcel and Louis Lavelle. As a matter of fact, B. Delfgaauw[1] is convinced that the Existentialism of Marcel is more characteristically French than that of Sartre. Delfgaauw writes: "If you desire to view the typical characteristics of French philosophy in all their sharpness, then you had better turn to the work of Louis Lavelle!" Delfgaauw mentions as such characteristics: the sobriety of his thought, the clarity of his expression and style, the harmony of his conception of the absolute and the human, and his great competence in science and art."

Louis Lavelle was born in 1883 and was appointed to fill the chair in philosophy left vacant by the famous philosopher, Henri Bergson.[2]

As one of the main figures in the movement known as the *Philosophie de l'esprit,* Lavelle has written books on

[1] *De Wijsbegeerte van Louis Lavelle,* in *Alg. Tijschrift voor Wijsbegeerte and Psychologie,* February, 1947, p. 75.

[2] Tr. note. Bergson died in 1941 as the victim of Nazi persecution. He refused to accept any special favors in his own behalf and accepted the restrictions imposed upon all Jews during this period. D.H.F.

metaphysics and ethics. On many points the system of
Lavelle is related to that of Marcel. Only in one respect
does Lavelle deviate from the latter. Marcel very consistently rejects all system, but Lavelle values a viewpoint
which is systematically constructed. In this respect he is
formally similar to Sartre.

According to Lavelle all philosophical problems are
included in one cardinal problem, namely, in *the analysis
of my original experience of Being.* "This conception of
philosophy is an argument for metaphysics."[1]

We shall now examine the way in which Lavelle con-
ducts this analysis. As all existentialists, Lavelle proceeds
upon the assumption that the essence of man cannot be
conceptualized. It cannot be defined in a concept because
human Existence precedes the essence of man. The essence of man cannot be defined, because as long as he
is on earth man is in a state of becoming. Because of his
transcending Existence man is ever on the way to himself.
To exist is to be in search of the essence of man. This
Existence occurs in self-transcendence and self projection;
it is realized by the choice of our own possibilities in un-
determined freedom.

Lavelle views this process of self-transcendence as
being based upon the fact that man stands in a relation
to the absolute Being of God. (In this respect, Lavelle's
view is related to that of Marcel; however, Lavelle prefers
to call God "The All.") Through this relation man is ever
furnished new possibilities.

The most fundamental experience of man is the *experience of Being.* This experience accompanies all our
acts and is in the background of all that we do. It is
always the same. Our experience of Being is always identical. What we think or do is in constant change, but the

[1] *Ibid.,* p. 80.

experience that I am the one who thinks or acts, is always the same. From this it follows that the Being which we encounter in every experience of Being is always a concrete specific Being. We never approach absolute Being directly. We approach it indirectly through specific Being or Existence. This absolute Being lies hidden behind all concrete Being. It is unconditional, without determination or reference.

The Being of everything which exists concretely is nothing other than the Being of God, The All. Outside of God there is nothing. Everything which exists must participate in the Being of God because God is Absolute Being. It is a contradiction in terms to think of the existence of any Being other than the Being of God. Such Being would be even greater than the Being of God, and the latter is absolute and all-inclusive.

Lavelle has lost sight of the primary principle of a Biblical ontology. A Christian ontology recognizes an essential distinction between the Being of God and everything which is not God, and everything which is not God is subject to the law of God. As all existentialists, Lavelle does not recognize divine law. Existentialists do not have any room for divine law, because in their thought man alone is his own sovereign law-giver. Existentialism is only free to choose between atheism and pantheism. Lavelle chooses the latter.

The only Being is the Being of God and the Being of all that exists is exclusively the Being of the All. Lavelle means by this that Being is *univocal* in character. All Being is of the same essence. There is no qualitative difference in Being. The Being of men and things, of properties and potentialities, of reality and illusion is always the same. Wherever we can speak of Being it is the Being of God, and there is no other sort of Being.

Yet even though there is only one Being which is

everywhere present, there is a difference between people, between God and things, and between various things. To account for this difference, Lavelle introduces the traditional distinction between *esse* and *essentia*, between *Being* and *essence*. In *esse*, Being, all beings are alike, but they differ in their essences, or in the determination of their Being. *Being* and *essence*, *esse* and *essentia*, are identical in God, but in all other forms of Existence they must be distinguished from each other.

From this it follows that on the one hand God is everything and in everything, and, on the other hand, not every specific Being is God. The difference is not that the various Beings are not God. If this were true then God would not be everything. All Beings are divine, but every specific thing is not itself God. The various forms of Being participate or share in God. Or otherwise stated: God realizes Himself in concrete things.

The character of the real divine Being is spirit, action, deed. The Being of God is *to exist*. God is identical with the *history of God*. Just as man creates himself, there is also a self-creation of God! We are here confronted by an existential idea of God.[1] Every Being that exists, that participates in the divine, exists through a divine act.

The concepts of a Creator and a creation are foreign to this system of thought. They are replaced by the concept of the absolute Being of God and the specific Being of concrete Existence which participates in God's Being. The concept of participation is central in Lavelle's conception. Specific Being cannot be created Being. If it were, the Being of things would add something to the Being of the Creator so that His Being would no longer be absolute.

By participation Lavelle means that something shares

[1] See: Dr. S. U. Zuidema: *De Mensch als historie*, p. 17.

in the Being of the All without becoming the All. Something is divine without itself being God. Such participation is only possible because the Divine Being acquires a limitation in things. This restriction is found in matter. We can only meaningfully speak of participation with respect to man. Philosophy is exclusively a human activity. We have knowledge of man from our own experience. We experience our own Being which stands in a relation to the absolute Being of God.

Does not this lead to solipsism, to the extreme consequence of individualism, to the doctrine that I am alone? No, for people other than myself experience their own Being. I do not know this on the basis of experience but on the basis of faith. Of things, in contrast, I know very little. I only know that my thinking encounters them as an uncrossable boundary. And as a matter of fact, I know that my thinking has itself called this boundary into existence. I can only say of things that they are appearances, they are phenomena.

My limited Being participates in the absolute Divine Being. This participation means that my Being is enclosed or curtailed by my body. If I was only Being then I would be absolute Being, I would be God. The fact that I am divine but not God is due to my body. My body is a thing, a phenomenon, matter. Human Existence is, therefore, twofold: on the one hand, it is spirit or thought, being or deed, and on the other hand, it is matter, thing, appearance. The second aspect of human Existence is a limitation of the first. Because of this limitation I am not identical with God. Thus, through the combination of these two moments, I am a Being that in a relative sense participates or shares in the Absolute. This participation, in other words, is the limitation of the Unlimited, the restriction of the Absolute.

Lavelle denies that man has any direct contact with

God. We can only come into contact with God by way of all that which is not-God. We can only approach Him who is the ground of all things via the things which are only the results of the first cause, *The All*.

Existence, self-transcendence, is possible through this contact with God. Man is on the way to his real Being in this continual transcendence of himself. Man approaches his essence by continually surpassing himself. He approaches his real Existence and is ever more himself, and man is what he becomes. Our Existence is on the one hand our determination; on the other, it is our calling; it is that which we must become, the unfolding of our potentialities.

This process of self-transcending is ontological in character because it is concerned with the actualization of a form of being which is my highest potentiality; on the other side this process is ethically characterized because the highest form of Being is at the same time the best and most valuable manner of Existence.

This highest form of Existence is not to be sought in the knowledge of all the things in the external world, nor is it to be found in the investigation of all the Being which is outside of my Existence. Rather it is to be found in the deepening of the relation which is between my limited Being and the Absolute Being of God. I do not discover *The All* by scattering myself in the diversity of the world. I discover it in the mysterious introspection of the Being of myself, in which I participate in God.

Does Lavelle mean by this that I must turn my back upon the world and seek my salvation in another worldly mystical attitude toward life? The answer is no. For Lavelle this existential contact with the absolute Being of God is the foundation for a real understanding of the world. It is the only adequate basis for life in the world.

The conception that the world is primarily the totality of concrete things is not correct. The real world is not material but spiritual in nature. It is the totality of all men with whom we stand in some sort of a relation. This spiritual world is primary. Only through the spiritual world does the material world of phenomena acquire meaning and significance. The meaning of the material world is that it draws a boundary between the many persons and separates them from each other. The material world of phenomena separates individuals in the same way that the body is the limitation of our Divine Being. The phenomena enable individuals to maintain communion with each other.

Things are always subordinate to persons and this state of affairs cannot be reversed. There is no doubt that persons exist, but the existence of things is problematical.

Actually Lavelle's conception of a thing is a puzzle. We can readily say that it is a stumbling block as it undeniably introduces an antinomy into his thought. Lavelle has clearly taught us that only man participates in the Being of God, and, God is the Real, the only Being. Ergo: There can be no Being which remains to be ascribed to a *thing*.

We can reach the same conclusion in another way. The *ontical* function of things or phenomena is to limit. But Being as such does not include any limitation. Ergo: things do not exist. Yet according to Lavelle things do exist. It is not clear however, how things can have a non-participating existence if God is the only Being. Nor is it clear how, as Beings, things can limit.

In any case, the place of man in the world is conceived by Lavelle as follows. Man is placed in the middle of the spiritual world of his fellow man in order to have intercourse and communion with him by means of things. Through this contact and communion, the contact with

God, the Absolute Being, is confirmed and strengthened, and this has the ethical consequence of personal purification, in order to strive consciously after this existential ideal of life. For this reason I must remove all disturbing influences, everything which takes my attention away from God. I must rather seek everything which advances my contact with God. In the final analysis, I must occupy myself with the one Being that reveals Himself, as the identical One, in the multiplicity of Existence.

All the motives of existential thought are present in Lavelle's conception. This includes, of course, the motive of the authentic and the unauthentic. For Lavelle Being is spirit, deed, freedom. In human Existence, however, this Being is limited by and bound to the body. The latter is material, passive, and determined. Therefore, there are two possible directions which are opposed to each other in human Existence. There is the authentic direction in which in full freedom the spirit seeks contact with *The All*. And in the other direction the human spirit is degraded to matter and freely permits itself to be shackled and determined. The decision in this conflict is made by the autonomous will of the free individual.

Lavelle's thought is a strong pantheistic reaction against the nihilistic atheistic thought of which Sartre is the popular prophet.

Our philosophical characterization of this system is nearly the same as that of Marcel. The system of Lavelle is that of a typical humanistic philosophy of freedom. It is orientated toward the religious motive of the ideal of personality and bears a definite irrationalist and subjective character. This irrationalism also culminates in personalism. And its subjectivism—in denying the law of God and in positing the freedom of man who himself establishes all law—is accompanied by an *individualism* that constructs society from the existential Being of the individual.

III

SARTRE

Jean Paul Sartre was born in 1905. He is the last French existentialist that we shall examine, and although the most popular, he is not the most typical existentialist philosopher. Besides being a philosopher, Sartre is the author of numerous literary works. As a philosopher, Sartre was a student of Heidegger and Husserl; however, DesCartes, Hegel, and Freud have also exercised an influence upon his thought. His philosophical method is an intertwining of the phenomenology of Husserl with the dialectic of Hegel.

Sartre's main philosophical work is entitled *L'Etre et le Neant* (1943) (*Being and Nothingness*). He has also written a brief summary of his thought in *Existentialism is a Humanism*. And just before the last war he wrote books on scientific psychology and on the phenomenology of Husserl.

Sartre's whole theory is built on the experience of finiteness and on the antithesis between what he calls *"en-soi,"* the *being-in-itself* of the material being of the world, and the *"pour soi,"* the *being for itself of human consciousness.*

As consciousness, Sartre characterizes subjective human being as the only source of value, and as completely free and responsible. This freedom, however, is purely arbitrary, because the only responsibility that exists is that which man has to himself. Man is the only measure of all value and all truth.

A strong vein of despair runs through the thought of Sartre. Human Existence is structurally determined as an *éschec,* a failure. In the last words of his main work he says that man is a *"passion inutile,"* a useless passion. And in addition to this he posits the contradictory nature of the essence of human consciousness. Human consciousness is on the one side finite and contingent, because of its appearance, but on the other hand, its activity is directed toward the pursuit of an Unapproachable Absolute. "The Absolute is in turn a contradition: Absolute-Being would mean to be the conscious source of everything that is; but while the absolute is a unity, consciousness is inseparable from a dualism (consciousness is always consciousness of something)."[1] Therefore, the final word concerning man is that: "Built as he is upon a contradiction, man exhausts himself in search of another contradiction."

To understand the preceding we must understand that according to Sartre the notion of the Absolute contains both being-in-itself, *en soi,* self-sufficiency, and consciousness, *pour soi.* However, this Absolute does not and cannot exist. For although the material being of the world has *en soi,* being-in-itself that is contingent and absurd, it does not possess consciousness. In addition, human consciousness seeks self-sufficiency, it seeks to realize the idea of God, but it does not and cannot reach this ideal. The ideal ever remains a phantom. For man as *pour soi,* as existential self-consciousness, is never himself, but always *BECOMES* himself. The human ideal is intrinsically contradictory. Therefore, our Existence is the striving after an illusion.

Another distinguishing feature of Sartre's philosophy is that he characterizes human subjectivity as *Nullity,* (nothingness). He arrives at this notion in the following manner. The idea of veritable being is being-in-itself, *en soi.* We find this *being-in-itself,* in a certain sense at

[1] Dr. A. de Waelhens: *De Franse wijsbegeerte tijdens en Sedert de oorloog,* in: *Alg. Ned. Tijdschrift voor Wijsb. en Psych.,* p. 125.

least,[1] in things, matter, but not in the ego, not in consciousness. (Our ego, consciousness, strives to become) being-in-itself, *en soi,* but it never reaches this end. Therefore, human subjectivity is *nullity, nothingness.*

We can reach this same conclusion in another way. Our consciousness renders the world unreal. Our consciousness of something places us outside of it. It we are conscious, for example, that a tree is outside of our window, the consciousness we have of the tree is not itself the tree. If the tree is a being, then the consciousness that we have of this being is non-being. Thus all consciousness of something is an escape from its reality; it is a knowledge that it is impossible for me to identify myself with the factuality of reality.

From this it follows that I can never make any pronouncement about myself or others. I can never specify any qualification about myself which would apply to the present. I can never identify myself or another with a certain quality. If, for example, I were to say that I am stingy, this affirmation would be incorrect. For in the act of consciousness, in which I am conscious of being stingy, I place myself outside of *stingyness.* The consciousness of stinginess is not being stingy itself. If in contrast I were to affirm that I am not avaricious, then I disavow the facts in which my avariciousness has clearly appeared. So this also is not true. Whoever affirms that he is bad, lies. For even if a person has been very bad in the past, no one—on account of his absolute freedom —is determined to remain bad. In the future he can exercise his freedom to act rightly. However, one must not

[1] This limitation, "in a certain sense," intends to convey the fact that it is going too far if we say that *"en soi"* is in itself and coincides with itself, because it solely "is." It "is": contingent, factual, absurd, without reason, without necessity, a "brute existent," a *"chaos original."* Thus writes S. U. Zuidema: *Nacht zonder dageraad,* p. 12 ff.

say that he is good. For what guarantee is there that you will remain good? Are you not always free to become bad?

These examples illustrate the fact that Sartre denies the possibility of uprightness, of *good faith*. For fidelity means that in the future we shall be the same as we are in the present. But such an identity is impossible for man. It would mean the negation of his freedom. Man is *not*, but he becomes. He transcends his factuality. He is always what he is not, and he is not what he is. The conclusion is that man is always and necessarily capricious.

Consequently, in the very nature of consciousness is implied the fact that each pronouncement concerning the essence of man is necessarily incorrect. Insofar as man is factuality, such a pronouncement is justifiable, but man is more than factuality. For in every moment he transcends his factuality in absolute freedom. What man shall become can never be determined.

Thus consciousness in-itself, *pour soi*, is not factuality, but a flight from it; it is a *nihilification*, the destruction of reality. It is *nothing, nullity*.

The existence of reality is necessarily proved from the presence of consciousness. The *en soi*, the real being of matter, is primary. Consciousness is secondary, because *pour soi* is the destruction and denial of the *en-soi*. Consciousness is always directed toward something. It is nothing but a relation with reality. Thus the existence of reality is included in the experience of consciousness.

Man has self-consciousness. But this also is a nihilification, a destruction. For in self-consciousness I am conscious that I am not myself. I am conscious that I transcend in freedom the factuality of my milieu, heredity, predisposition, character, and so on. It follows from this that self consciousness arises indirectly via reality. Sartre definitely denies the existence of an inner man, a "pure" or transcendental consciousness that is abstracted from external reality. There is no consciousness as a pure possession of the self. All consciousness is transcendent as the destruction of factuality. On the one hand factuality is a hindrance to the freedom of consciousness, and on the other hand factuality is its point of departure.

Sartre is a convinced atheist. Many philosophers merely deny the existence of God and do not take God into account in their thinking. But this is not the case with Sartre. His very philosophical conception is built upon the impossibility of the existence of God. His thought is intentionally and brutally opposed to God. And, Sartre maintains that even if God were to exist nothing would be changed in the world.

Sartre has a twofold reason for his denial of the existence of God. In the first place the idea of God is an illusion because it is intrinsically contradictory. If God were to exist, he would not only be a *pour soi*, a conscious subject, an Existence, but he would at the same time be an *en-soi*, someone Who is his own foundation and Who rests self-sufficiently in Himself. But these two determinations are incompatible. For to be a *pour-soi* is to exist, it is becoming; and an *en-soi* is being which does not become. Therefore, there is no God.

And in the second place the idea of God is in conflict with the idea of true humanity. Sartre wishes to be a humanist and he desires to bring humanism to its logical conclusion. The essence of the idea of humanity is the full freedom of man. Man is autonomous. He is responsible to himself alone and is the creator of his own law and norm. If man is to gain his freedom and autonomy, the idea of God cannot be tolerated. If the idea of God is seriously considered, human freedom can never be absolute. Human freedom requires, therefore, the death of God. The death of God is its necessary corollary.

Moreover, if humanism is to be consistently carried out, it is not enough to abolish the idea of God. We must also abandon any notion that man is dependent upon laws or norms which exist outside of himself. There are no eternal rational truths or anything similar to them. Rationalism had made the mistake of believing in such eternal truths. In this respect rationalism seems to have been infected by the Christian faith, which teaches the doctrine of the divine order of creation which precedes man and to which man is subject.

A fact especially worthy of careful attention is that Sartre, as an atheist, rejects in principle all the motives of Christianity which are connected with the Christian faith. Yet, and this is what merits attention, his own system is not free from Christian motives. The latter are secularized in Sartre, they return in his system in another context.

Sartre denies the Christian belief that God is the free all powerful Creator of all things. Yet, by attributing creative power to man, Sartre predicates to man this very idea of creation. Man not only creates his own law by his absolute power, but through his absolutely free deeds, man is also the creator of the world. In Sartre's conception subjectivism reaches its zenith and culminates in an *absolute subjectivism.*

In this fashion Sartre thinks that he has saved human responsibility. According to Sartre, the person who believes in a God who has created all things and to Whom he is subject, flees from his own freedom and responsibility. Real freedom is the absolute arbitrariness of man. Man is outside of law and in his deeds only reckons with himself. True responsibility is to be responsible to oneself and to no one else.

With respect to society, Heidegger had recognized a *mit-sein* (being-together) that is one of the essential characteristics of human Existence. Because of his absolute subjectivism, Sartre differs with his teacher and does not have room in his thought for an authentic *living-together*. The essence of society for Sartre is conflict and struggle.

Every other person has the same unlimited freedom that I have. Consequently, the freedom of other people is necessarily a threat to my own freedom. It is an attack upon my own autonomy. In my own free sphere I move about without consideration for others. I act purely arbitrarily. If anyone were to respect my freedom he would at the same time have to abandon his own. My neighbor can only feel the urge to destroy my freedom if he is to answer the call to fulfill his own freedom. What we have said applies to everyone. "Thus my neighbor is for me the devil, and life in social relations with others is similar to the fall into sin."[1]

Sartre's absolute subjectivism goes hand in hand with a complete individualism, and the latter necessarily results in a rejection of all authority in social relationships and in principle ends in anarchism.

There has been a heated debate between Marxists and Sartre. The Marxists have accused Sartre of being "the last witness of bourgeois decadence, entirely caught in subjective despair." Sartre answered this accusation quite vehemently as he is jealous to maintain the revolutionary character of his doctrine. Sartre shares the view of the Marxists with respect to the essence, rôle, and future of bourgeois and capitalist society; but he is of the opinion that a theory which is based on a theory of determinism cannot be revolutionary. "Only a philosophy of absolute freedom and self-determination can claim to be revolutionary." In reply the Marxists answered, "A person cannot attain any goal with a freedom that makes each man the judge of his own ends." Moreover, the Marxists maintain that Sartre is not able to check despair and chaos and

[1] *Ibid.*, p. 10.

shall finally appear as the vanguard of a new fascism."[1]
This controversy is conducted in the camp of subjectivism.
Sartre is an individualist and Marxists are universalists.

According to Sartre the presence of our neighbor
tempts us to abandon a life in which we exercise our
freedom. It tempts us to cast away our own responsibility
and to sacrifice ourselves to public opinion by placing our
own responsibility upon the shoulders of the masses. We
feel protected and comfortable if we live, think, and act
as *everyone* does. But wherever man is resolved in society
and becomes a part of a community he betrays his own
freedom and becomes a part of the mass.

This is the origin of the idea of God. God is the hypostatization, the deification of public opinion, of the masses,
of collectivity. If a person flees from his own freedom
and betrays his own responsibility by living according
to the judgment of society or in the presence of God, then
this person is guilty of *bad faith* because he is unfaithful
to himself. This bad faith is the death blow to true humanity. Religion is equal to a fall into sin; it is an aliena-
tion and loss of self!

What is for Sartre the ideal of human Existence?
Deification, man must become as God! The deepest passion of man is to become free from all connection with
matter. He must detach himself from his own body and
become separate from the world which surrounds and
stifles him. The goal of man is to become self-sufficient.
He must become his own foundation and rest in himself.
Man must constitute himself as God and thus be his own
highest good.

With this is related the fact that the basic attitude
which controls man is that of *nausea*. What is it that dis-
gusts man? Man is disgusted and nauseated by the inflex-

[1] Prof. A. De Waelhens: *De Franse wijsbegeerte tijdens en sedert de
oorloog.* in *Alg. Ned. Tijdschrift voor wijsbegeerte en Psych.*, p. 126.

ibility and massiveness of the material being of the world. "This nausea can suddenly come over me in an unexplainable way. Without any warning everything gets dim and I am choked with disgust. It seems as though I am caught in a whirlpool and blending together with all the things around me I am drawn down and I am no longer myself. I am swept away by the being which is around me. There is no longer any distance between me and *things*. I feel the loss of my freedom. It is only possible for me to regain my freedom and to once again become myself if I can again acquire some distance between myself and the suffocating massiveness of being."[1]

With respect to his deification, man is in his absolute freedom, the creator, and as such, the ground of his own law, the source and the foundation of all value in his life. The only thing that man lacks is that he is not the foundation of himself. He does not rest in himself in divine self-sufficiency. The reason for this is that he is existentially bound to the *en soi*, the being of things, which is determined in itself. The highest human ideal is to become what he lacks, namely, to become his own foundation, to rest in himself. His ideal is not only to exist as *pour soi*, as someone who is responsible to himself in a life for himself, but his ideal is to be simultaneously an *en soi*, to be his own source and foundation, in short, to be like God.

The apostate character of this philosophy is clearly evident in this self worship. The philosophy of Sartre is a pseudo-religion. The self is served instead of a God. In the Biblical narrative in Genesis the devil portrayed this demonical idea as something attainable. Sartre confesses, in contrast, that this ideal is an illusion; we already know his argument. The *pour-soi* is the existential Existence that in permanent self-constituting is never itself, but al-

[1] Dr. C. A. Van Persen: *Korte inleiding in de Existentie-philosophie,* p. 27.

ways becomes itself. The *en-soi*, in contrast, is foreign to all becoming because it simply is. *En-soi* is simply there contingently, in all its meaninglessness, as an original chaos. For this reason *pour-soi* can never really be identical with *en-soi*. In this deification man searches after a fiction, a phantom. Man's life is irrevocably marked by failure. He lives in a tragedy of *éschec*.

In Sartre's thought there is no longer any trace of the optimistic view of culture and of man which was prevalent in rationalism. Human life is without hope and future. It is made up of continual unrest. Man is autonomous. He reaches after the highest goal, to become like God. In creative freedom he seeks to realize himself, yet man has no future. His life is like a night without a dawn.

From the Christian point of view, the tragedy in this pessimistic conception is that the wisdom of the world, ending here in the night of despair, will not listen to the Word of God which in ancient times stated that the Godless have no peace. "To the law and to the testimony: if they speak not according to this word, it is because there is no light in them." (Isaiah 8:20*)

The self deification of man is an illusion. But man does not break with this illusion even after he is aware of its fictitious character. Rather he continues to pursue this illusion in order to give meaning and value to his life in creative freedom.

As *pour-soi*, as a being for himself, man cannot become an *en-soi*, a self-sufficient being. Therefore, man is doomed to *extase*, that is to say, he must step outside of himself in order to come in contact with the contingent being of his body and of the world. He must transcend himself and become himself. He must ever exist and ever approach his unattainable idea to be like God. Sartre's well known definition of Existence is *L'existence precede l'essence*, Existence precedes the essence. By this is meant that we can never say what a person is, because he is always in a process of *becoming*. The term essence includes in its connotation the notion that man is subject to laws, rules, and fixed norms to which he more or less responds. Existentialism has radically broken with such a view. Man is nothing because he exists. His Existence precedes his essence, because as free creating subjectivity, man is also the origin of his own law, rule, and meaning. In his deepest meaning man is lawless. Every law that he posits, he sets forth in absolute free power. He posits it for himself in his own sovereign good pleasure.

This human Existence is unknowable to rational reflection. Yet, it is not unknowable. Knowledge of human Existence precedes all rational self reflection. It is acquired by intuition, and all men are endowed with such an intuitive self knowledge of our existential subjectivity.

In this intuition, every person discovers for himself that in its very roots his subjectivity is *freedom.* This freedom is the source of a continual choice of the self to rule over oneself in free decisions. This freedom is without any limits. It is determined by nothing; it is infinite and inaccessible. In freedom sovereign man is always related to himself. He transcends himself in every free decision that he makes. Man is never what he is and he is always what he is not. From this it follows that man cannot be defined. Each definition of him is incorrect because there is nothing identical or constant in man. We cannot say what he is and we cannot say what he will become. By means of this freedom man isolates himself from himself. He continually renders himself unreal. In consequence it is utterly impossible to speak of a human nature. For this would imply that all men act in accordance with fixed patterns which are not susceptible to change.

On account of this freedom man is endowed with a *responsibility* which consists in being responsible to oneself in duty to oneself and not to anything else. There is nothing outside of man to which man owes allegiance. By nature a person is neither good or bad, because, in full responsible freedom, each person chooses virtue or vice for himself. All psychical determinism is from the devil. No factor outside of a person's own will ever dooms him to follow a certain course. No external condition modifies his behaviour in any way. Each person could have taken another course or have chosen another way to act.

It is not impossible, however, for someone to abandon his call to freedom. In fact most people are guilty of this very thing. The large masses of humanity flee from their own freedom by subjecting themselves to various laws and norms which society legislates for those who are afraid of their own freedom. It is nevertheless impossible for man to escape entirely from his own freedom. He cannot completely destroy his own absolute subjectivity but is prevented from doing so by *Angst*. In *Angst*, human subjectivity reveals itself to itself.

Thus man is free and responsible to himself alone. He is the sole origin of all value and norm in human Existence. He creates the meaning of life and of the whole world. For outside of free human Existence, being is meaningless, chaotic, and absurd.

In the Humanism of Sartre, freedom is opposed in an absolute manner, to the absurdity and meaninglessness of nature. This Humanism is intrinsically connected with nihilism. This highly esteemed human subjectivity existentially strives to attain the ideal of deification in free self determination. But this subjectivity is nothingness, it lacks any ontological character. It only exists because of its relation to nature. Even our body belongs to nature. The being of nature has an ontical precedence over the non-being of our consciousness. Non-being is based upon being.

This nihilism is consequently the counterpole of all

idealism that still ascribes positive being to the human spirit.

This nihilist view of human personality undermines one of the very foundations of Humanism. The Existentialism of Sartre signifies a crisis in Humanism because nihilism gnaws at the root of the ideal of personality.

Sartre is a materialist in his ontology, theory of being. For the only being which he recognizes is nature, matter. The character of being is ascribed to matter alone. Nature is the only factual being, and as such it is inviolable. Factual being is not abandoned to illusion or to nothingness.

All Existence which is other than human consciousness belongs to factual being. Everything belongs to it which is not the product of the free acts of our absolute subjectivity. Factual being is independent of human consciousness. The converse of the preceding statement, however, is not true. It is not the case that human subjectivity can exist apart from nature, for I become conscious only when I separate myself from factual being. Consciousness only arises as the result of my distinguishing myself from factual being in my awareness that I am not factual being. To arrive at the distinction between the primary independent being of nature and the secondary non-being of human subjectivity, Sartre employs the concept of *en-soi* and *pour-soi*. As we have already stated, *en-soi* is being that is enclosed within itself and is identical with itself, and *pour-soi*, is being-for-itself, self-transcending Existence.

En-soi, the chaotic and meaningless being of nature, is not related to itself, it does not *exist*, it does not transcend itself. *En-soi* is only there, without reason, without cause, only by chance. It also exists outside of time. Nature is eternal. Human consciousness, in contrast, *nothingness* (nullity), exists in time. For human consciousness accepts the factuality of itself in the past, it is present with itself in the present, and projects itself into the future.

Eternal matter is contingent and without value. It must receive its meaning and value from human subjectivity which cannot exist without matter. Nevertheless, human subjectivity transcends itself and in relation to nature pursues the illusory idea of God.

By saying that matter is contingent we mean that it does not owe its origin to the principle of freedom of the human spirit.

Now what is the scope of this being of nature? To it Sartre ascribes everything which is non-human, the world of things, plants, and animals. However, in addition, he also includes under the being of nature, the body of man and everything which belongs to the past of our human consciousness and was once the fruit of our free decision. Everything that has happened is deposited in the great receptacle of contingent being, because it no longer is subject to the power of freedom. We no longer have any choice with respect to that which is factual. The past is unchangeable. When man dies he reverts completely to this contingent and absurd being. Existence and becoming cease at death, and only matter remains. Death extinguishes freedom and terminates *nothingness*.

We have seen that Sartre reckoned the past of man and his body to contingent being. He now identifies the past of man with his body. We cannot exceed our body. It is the necessary form of our human contingency and it is indispensable for the realization of the freedom of our consciousness. The fact that we accept our body is also a deed of our own freedom.

An important part of our freedom is limited by the factuality of our body. In addition, our freedom is limited by the contingency of our situation. We are surrounded by nature. We act in a society and our path is contingently crossed by our fellowman. Thus very little actually remains of the absolute character of our freedom. What is man according to Sartre? S. U. Zuidema gives this dreary comfortless answer, from which appears the truth of the statement once made to the effect that Existentialism is the grave digger of Western European culture. "His origin is absurd, his Existence is absurd, and his end is absurd. And the non-absurd of human Existence exists within this relentless horizon of absurdity. The non-absurd of human Existence consists of the meaningless ascription of meaning to an unchangeable absurd reality. And this ascription is made by a freedom which chooses itself."[1]

We can be brief in our characterization of Sartre's conception. As that of other existentialists, his system is *individualistic, irrationalistic, subjectivism*. It is superfluous for us to say more.

Certain features distinguish Sartre from his fellow existentialists: atheism in his theory of God, nihilism in his view of the human spirit, and materialism in his theory of being that is reduced to nature. Our exposition of these points is sufficient to permit us to terminate our discussion of Sartre.

In conclusion, we need only note that Sartre's nihilistic anthropology is the kernel of his system, and this anthropology strikes a death blow at the heart of Humanism and of Existentialism.

[1] Zuidema, *op. cit.*, p. 30.

CHAPTER IV

THE THEISTIC EXISTENTIALISM
OF LOEN

THE theological-philosophical Existentialism of Loen[1] is often neglected. In my opinion, however, the unusual and genial conception disclosed by Loen in his work *De Vaste grond* (1946), merits our full attention and consideration. I am not interested in Loen because I believe that he will advance Christendom in its interpretation of the world in the light of the Bible. I am interested in him because I believe his system is attractive to many who are infected by the spirit of Karl Barth and seek to effect a synthesis with the irrationalistic spirit of the time.

What is unusual about Loen's view is its synthetic character. It attempts to effect a synthesis between the Christian faith and motives of modern Existentialism. It offers us a philosophy which—because of its theological starting-point—takes God and His Word very seriously, and at the same time thinks it has conquered all non-Christian philosophy. Theologically Loen's position is orientated toward the position of Barth, and it can be

---

[1] Arnoldus Ewout Loen, born in 1896, is an extremely gifted individual. At present he is the director of a *Rijks Hoogere Burgerschool* in the Netherlands. In addition to being an engineer, he has received a graduate degree in mathematics and natural science and has published a Ph.D. thesis in philosophy, entitled, *Philosophy and Reality (Wijsbegeerte en werkelijkheid)*. His main work, *De Vaste Grond* (1946) a systematic exposition of his existentialist conception, was followed by an *Introduction to Philosophy (Inleiding tot de Wijsbegeerte* (1947).

Loen is a congenial systematic thinker, and in spite of similarities between his point of view and that of Karl Barth, Jaspers, and N. Hartmann, his starting point and his thought bear witness to fresh originality.

readily seen that it derives philosophical motives from Jaspers, Heidegger, Marcel, and N. Hartmann. Nevertheless, Loen is not an eclectic, but, motivated by an original vision, he systematically and consistently develops his starting point.

In this section we shall give a summary and critique of his position.

The *Theory of the Word* comprises the first part of his point of view. Philosophical impulse is the motivation to find the *ground or basis of Existence* (that is human being as *Existence*) and of the world. We can only speak of rational insight into this ground if the ground itself belongs to the sphere of reason or logos. But if God is the ground of Existence and of the world then it is not permitted to seek this ground in human thought or in the autonomy of human Existence.

God reveals Himself in His Word, that is, in Jesus Christ. Revelation is not an announcement of truth, but God's creative voice in the present by which He calls man and the world into existence. Man is a self in the face of God and his neighbor, a self endowed with freedom by which he can place himself in relation to God. The Word of God does not only create man in the present, as the hearer of the Word, but it also creates the *situation* of the hearer; that is to say, he must answer. The answer we give to the Word of God is also creative, because it intervenes in our situation. No one can escape answering.

Christ is the Word of God become flesh. He is God and man. God speaks to Himself in Christ and in Him gives an answer to Himself. In this answer of Christ the Word of God comes to us. In His answer God is obedient to the Word. Therefore, He establishes in His answer a fellowship between Himself and us. This communion had been broken by our answer. Christ reestablishes this fellowship, and gives us a share in His answer.

Thought and action is our *self-realization,* in which we translate possibility into reality. If Existence is vexed and annoyed with the Word of God, then it seeks its own possibility and believes that it can be its own ground. What is assimilated into Existence in free self realization is *concrete.* The concrete is *not* but becomes.

The Word of God, Jesus Christ, is concrete in the Holy Spirit. The concreteness of the Word is its creating. God creates and recreates us as hearers of His Word through His Holy Spirit. In our disobedience the Word creates concretely as rejection and judgment. Opposed to the concreteness of the judging Word is the concreteness of the freely speaking Word in the Holy Spirit. God recreates us by the Word of Redemption. This is the wonder of the Holy Spirit. God's grace is the daily ascription by the Holy Spirit of the answer that God gave in Christ.

There is a twofold history. The *real* history is that of the Word. In opposition to it stands *"our"* disqualified history, which is involved in a crisis with respect to the Word. It is marked by a "vacuity of events," as rebellion against God. However, God's grace through the Word will sanctify "our" history so that it participates in the history of God.

Insofar as Jesus Christ is an historical figure, He is not the Word of God. God's Word projects itself in the plane of human world-orientation as a wonder. God's Word has its own historicity, related to its eternity. . .

Between creation and the completion of the world, the history of the Word stretches itself out, with its great *incisions* (caesuren): creation, sin, atonement, redemption, and completion.

God chooses for His history the same stage as that

upon which our own history is played. Our history is in the history of the Word the period of sin. Through the resurrection of Christ our history stands under the promise that God creates something new.

The present is the eternity of the Word, that today creates us as existing people, as sinners, as reconciled, as redeemed, and as those who have hope of being perfected. The present is the presence of God, who reveals Himself in His Word, it is the actuality of eternity. In this present the whole history of the Word is present.

Eternity is in God the origin of time. What is specific in the concept of eternity is a relation to time. Our time which is created by God is the time of sin and death. In its determination by the judgment for sin our Existence is a being-toward-the-end (sein-zum-ende, zum-Tode). In Christ we have eternal life, the life out of and to the eternal God. Our time is then the time of life, God's time.

Our Existence, but also the essence (wezen), the *being-thus* of Existence and world, are the content of the creating Word that is spoken today. According to God's intention, creation must give answer to His Word. If it does not give this answer, then creation falls under the judgment of death. Creation is in its foundation apostate and does not answer to its goal. Therefore, Christ became a creature in order to recreate creation.

Creation is the origin of the history of the Word. The Word of the divine creation cries out: I love you, therefore, you may love Me and your neighbor. This is not a *command* but a *gift*. It became a command only after the entrance of sin.

In this situation in which we may give an answer we are *free*. The image of God lies in this freedom. This is the freedom of potentiality, of twofold possibility. The second sort of freedom is that of the *actus*, of the actual response to our essence, the freedom of returning love to God.

78

We have misused our freedom by rejecting the love of God. This is our sin, our apostasy, which is without any motive. Even though the sinner intends to establish his own Existence by being independent and free from God, by the rejecting of the love of God, the sinner really *negates* his own Existence.

Sin is only disclosed in the face of God's judgment and command; it is thus only revealed in the light of the Word. Therefore, sin belongs to the history of the Word. In freedom we have chosen death, but we are not free to prevent God from speaking further, namely, in the Word of reconciliation.

Sin which desecrates God's justice requires satisfaction, death, and condemnation. God Himself has borne this condemnation and has Himself experienced death. This is the reconciliation that He has created.

Confronted by sin, God did not remain unchanged, but willed to enter into an event. Thus, God became *history*. In the Atonement he entered *time* which he had created. The Atonement is, therefore, the middle point of the history of The Word.

The *Command* of God includes both the judgment pronounced with respect to sin before the Atonement, and the demonstration of God's love and patience after the Atonement. This *Command* is the repetition of the Word of creation as an imperative after the entrance of sin. Through the divine *Command* we who are under judgment are today called into Existence. We can only speak of sin as atoned sin, and we can only speak of the *Command* as a *Command* which has not been obeyed.

Atonement is the Cross of Christ. God took our condemnation upon Himself and died. Redemption is the resurrection of Christ, an *inner* movement of God. It is a return of the Son to the Father, by which we are saved, reestablished as children of God, and made possessors of the faith that the Spirit works in us. The Holy Spirit *prays, believes, hopes, and has love for us*. However, we cannot localize our redemption in our "time." It occurs in the present as a repetition of the redemption which once occurred. There is a predestination of redemption. Is there also an election to reprobation? Loen answers that God has included all among the disobedient so that he could show his mercy to everyone.

The Kingdom of Christ will come with His second coming as the *completion* of the history of the Word. At the present time the external organization of the Church is closed to the world, and its closed character belongs to the very essence of the Church. However, this barrier must be broken down; it is in conflict with the law of the Kingdom. The completion of history will be accompanied by the destruction of this world of sin and death.

The theory of The Word is followed by the *theory of existence, existentiology*. God is; while Existence *is being-there* in the face of the Word of God.

Existence is appearing in the state of *being-there (Dasein)* as an answer to the Word of God. What appears in the *Dasein* (being-there) is the *Ego;* what is established in the *Dasein* according to the answer to the Word of God is the *Self*. The inner dialectic of Existence is the identification of the Ego and the Self. There is a twofold identification, namely, the one brought about by the Ego and the other by God.

The *incisions* of the Word determine corresponding incisions of Existence which are bound to an historical unity, a derived historicity.

God's Word is the expressed utterance of God's Being. The Word creates its content, The Word creates Existence in the situation of being able to answer, and it also creates the world and human history. There is a distance between God's Word and the Bible. They are not identical.

80

The Word of God guarantees its being heard. Existence knows of its situation by means of an existential knowledge, an intuitive knowledge. Existence in its actualization is the answer. The offense of the Word is an attempt to render the "Self" independent and to drive the Word out of the present. As a hearer of the Word, Existence gains *entrance into the present*. It finds itself, the world, and its neighbor in the present. The definiteness of the present is the being-thus of Existence as it acquires this determination out of the past. The focusing of Existence upon its present determination is its *disposition*.

Existence must give an answer to the specific content of the present. God listens to this answer and directs Himself to it in His subsequent utterances. God's speaking is in every present moment an individual word. The present is related to the Word of atonement and redemption; it is the *present of grace*. The duration of the present is the creation to perfection. The Word is present in the present in all of its incisions. The present is the present of the community of which the individual is a member.

In the present, Existence is called to redemption by the Word of Life. If this word is accepted then entrance into life is something else than death. The answer of Existence ought to be: here I am. In this answer lies the origin of the Ego of man.

It is God's daily faithfulness which *establishes* the self *in time*. Upon this depends the continuity of the Ego—which is free to accept or reject the Word.

In its rejection of the Word, the Ego is established in the *time of death*, in solitude. But through the Word of redemption the self is established in the *time of life*. Here is the continuity of redemption through the Holy Spirit. There is a discontinuity between the redeemed and a sinner. In redemption, however, as a member of the Church of Christ, one is together with his neighbor.

Existence is also a *being-there* (Dasein) in the world. The world is the environment of Existence. Sinful Existence strives according to its freedom as a power over the world, but it becomes a part of the world. It is lost in a meaningless world and is engulfed by itself. Culture is the self-development of Existence, a realization of its possibilities.

The one, indivisible Existence, unfolds itself in *modes of being,* namely, as disposition (entrance into the present), as action (establishment in time), and as knowing (being in the world). The principle of knowledge of the world is *observation.* The world of Existence is the world which Existence itself makes and earns. The world, which shares in the independence of Existence in opposition to the word, is the fallen creation. Redemption is the severance of solidarity with the world.

Existence flees from the situation of the spoken word in triviality of *workaday life.* It flees from redemption and exchanges the Word for Christendom as the content of culture. The common, every day life of *tittle tattle* is a life ruled by conventional norms in which society finds rest. This fleeing Existence is condemned as sin by the Word and is overcome by authentic daily life.

As an object in the world, the body does not belong to Existence. Being in the body introduced a foreign element in the self for itself. Existence is spirit, not flesh. Corporality is the basis of the being in the world.

The historical dimension of Existence exists under the ground category: the *being-there* in opposition to the Word. Here is accomplished the rendering independent of the self in opposition to the Word as an answer of Existence. In opposition to The Word the self here gives an answer from the depths of its Existence which renders the self independent. The ego can only be itself by responding to the love of God. If it does not make this response then the ego is not itself. The ground duality of this independence is thus: to be oneself or not to be oneself. We stand on the wrong side of this duality. We are inclosed in ourselves, and are not ourselves.

The will, within which being is not itself, is not a free will, but the forced repetition of the original will to be a will which is not itself.

We cannot know whether survival is possible under the uncovered wrath of God, because judgment is not applied to us in the present. Judgment is either suspended or annihilated in Christ. God's judgment is that He creates the sinner, the apostate man. Judgment is only made concrete by the Holy Spirit as an abrogated judgment. *The-being-which-is-not-the-self* of the self is established in time by the judgment. This *being* becomes independent and callous in opposition to the Word.

In the atonement God bore our rejection. It is impossible to become independent in opposition to the atonement. The ego cannot accept or reject the atonement. Here Existence itself is at an end: the old man is no longer. God's possibility and reality is the absolutely new man.

In His commandments God holds man accountable for the past and pleads with the sinner to allow himself to be reconciled. Existence does not wish to accept the atonement, this is the offense. But the offense is not the winner. The *being-self* of the ego cannot hold out. The way of God is successful.

Redemption is the resurrection from the dead. It is the end of independence, a transposing into life; it is to be redeemed and to become a part of the redeemed. Love and faith enter here through the Holy Ghost as God's love and faith. Existence in redemption is to partake of God's love. The wonder of the resurrection is that this new Existence is still itself *in-being-in-God's-love*. Existence is now a being-there in the Word, in Christ, in the Spirit. The temporal period of God's Kingdom is the period of the daily redemption and reconciliation, the period of the daily suffering of God. The theory of being follows:

Two questions are raised: What is Existence, that is, what is *that which exists?* and what is the *mode of being of that which exists?*

That which exists is that which erects itself, that which is independent of knowledge and of Existence. The *"is"* or *being of that which exists* is the wonder of the fundamental expressed *utterance* of *that which exists*. By His creating speech God gives expression to *that which exists*.

That which exists is not homogeneous but is articulated. Our knowledge, as the factual expression of *that which exists,* must be distinguished from God's creating *utterance of that which exists*. That is to say, it must be distinguished from the ontical utterance of God.

The categories are forms of the *utterance of that which exists. That which exists* is conceptual. It can be articulated in concepts because it proceeds from the Logos. The ground category is that of being; the remaining categories are specifications of *that which exists*.

Our factual *being-there* (Dasein) stands in need of being. Existence clamours for being which it does not have itself. This being of Existence, this ground of Existence, is God. The being of Existence, is, in relation to the real being, *established-being*.

In its expressed utterance, being is *truth*. God's being is the self establishing origin. God, the Being, is not a Person. He is solely expression, truth.

Being outside of God is the creation of his Word.

Existence does not establish itself, it is not established as independent. The spoken love of God is the being of Existence. Sin is the rendering independent of Existence. It is to want to be as God.

The world also has a limited independence from being, another being than that of Existence, namely, a being as *object*.

Non-being does not have any being, but is the opposite to the truth of being. Reality and appearance are not a part of being, but of knowing.

Truth is the expression of being. Being is the bearer of truth. Truth is not external with respect to being. In truth, being expresses itself as it is. Being is expressed in the various categories, and is at the same time expressed and mystery.

In the creation there are two spheres: Existence and the world. Existence is the Dasein (being-there) of an individual ego. The being of the world has a certain hypothetical character.

In the world there are various spheres of objectivity. We do not know if these spheres are *ontical* because we cannot give any positive specification of the bearer or bearers of the world.

Individuality belongs to the constant alien character of all which exists. The truth of knowing does not reach individuality but only the essence of that which exists.

The Dasein of Existence is one *ontical* sphere with many *individual bearers*.

The *pride* which seeks to be as God belongs to the essence of Culture. Religion is under the judgment as the desire of apostate Existence for God. Culture lives in the hope that it will be emancipated and attain the freedom of the children of God. Existence and the world, as two *ontical* spheres, are united by psychical action and organic life.

Finally, we shall present several ideas of Loen's theory of knowledge. Knowing is a relation between the knower and what is known. That which exists is independent of its being known. It precedes knowledge.

Knowledge is a modus of Existence (Being). Knowledge is *a participation in the truth of that which exists,* in *ontical* truth. The categories in which that which exists is known are *ontical* categories. Knowledge rests upon the faith that it is an approximation of ontical categories. God's redeeming love is the ground of the possibility of knowledge. The categories are received in the hearing of the Word.

The goal of knowledge is that which exists. Truth is not that which exists, but a character of being. *The being-known* of *that which exists* occurs in the hearing of truth. Truth is not known, but *that which exists* is known.

Ontical truth is the speaking of God. *Cognitive truth* is the realization of the participation in *ontical* truth. The knowing process seeks to express *ontical* truth, but *cognitive* truth is inadequate with respect to the *ontical.* Cognitive truth approaches the essence alone and is not suitable to grasp individuality which remains alien to it. Ontical truth is timeless, eternal. *Cognitive* truth arises in time.

The characteristics of knowledge are: 1. It is discursive, it traverses the sphere of truth; 2. it is concerned with the identity of *that which* is; 3. it is ever on the way from provisional to complete knowledge; 4. the *ontical* truth is a harmonious unity free from contradiction; 5. the knowing process converges toward *ontical* truth; 6. the knowing process begins upon the basis of categories which are given to us; 7. knowledge belongs to our life, it is a *living knowledge.*

The participation of science is an observation which presupposes hearing. The basic science is theology, the theory of the Word. The pure *science* of Existence is existentiology. In addition there are many sciences in the world; however, logic is related to all sciences because it investigates the general structure of the uttered expression of that which exists. And what about philosophy? Since God is the *fast ground* and theology is the science about this ground, philosophy is then the science of the grounded *being of that which is* in the ground (God). Philosophy is thus dependent upon theology.

This finishes our summary of Loen's theistic Existentialism. Whether or not it is Christian can only be answered after we have critically examined this system. We shall vary our method in dealing with Loen by now presenting our criticism of him.

To criticize Loen's Existentialism is difficult because his system is decidedly a *synthesis-philosophy* composed of non-Christian philosophical motives which are united with motives derived from the Bible.

The very divisions of Loen's philosophy clearly reveal the synthetic-character of his conception. In Loen we encounter the Biblical motives of the Trinity, revelation, creation, sin, atonement, and so on. Moreover, these motives are frequently argued with the aid of Bible texts.

The fact that Loen rejects the automony of human reason as the starting point of philosophy is to be commended from our point of view. Loen is on good ground in his recognition of a super-theoretical religious starting point, a commitment of faith, that lies at the foundation of philosophy. Also Loen will not hypostatize any non-rational *datum* of temporal reality, such as life or feeling. He will not permit such a datum to be made absolute in order to derive all of reality from it. On the contrary, it is his intention to construct a radical Christian system of philosophy on the basis of John's prologue: "In the beginning was the Word and the Word was with God and the Word was God."

He strikes a sympathetic note, therefore, when he writes: "If the Lord is not God, then there are many lords that we can serve: reason, life, Existence, being in essential quality, positive fact, humanity, natural law or culture, society, pure thought, feeling, or religion can then be served. There can be only one ground or foundation, and this philosophy must posit as absolute. But if the Lord is God, how can there be any other ground besides him?"[1] This is the one side of the synthesis. There is another aspect which is just as real in Loen's conception. This other side is Existentialism. Its typical characteristics, the existential idea of the becoming of self, the idea of freedom, the cleft between Existence and world, the antithesis between authentic and unauthentic Existence, intuition for existential knowledge, and so on, are all present in Loen's thought.

In every case of synthesis philosophy, Biblical and the non-Biblical motives are mutually exclusive. The former achieve their validity in the Christian faith, and the latter are derived from systems which maintain the autonomy of human reason and reject any apriori of faith.

Therefore, if a synthesis is to have any meaning, the motives of one group must dominate and devour those of the other. It is theoretically possible that the motives derived from the Bible play such a dominating role that they denature the non-Biblical motives by robbing them of their original meaning and incorporating them as terms with a new content. The opposite is also possible, namely that the apostate motives denature the Biblical motives by robbing them of their original meaning and giving them a new significance foreign to revelation.

[1]*Inleiding tot de wijsbegeerte*, p. 183.

Which one of these possibilities do we encounter in Loen's system? Is existentialist terminology only the instrument for intrinsically Biblical ideas, or have the concepts of Existentialism impressed their stamp upon the motives derived from the Bible?

The answer is indisputable. Undoubtedly the latter possibility is the case. Existentialism has overcome the Biblical motives and burdens them with a system of thought which at root is foreign to revelation. Thus, Prof. Zuidema can write: "This theory of revelation or *Logology* is at once familiar and foreign to a Bible believing Christian. It desires to be extremely orthodox; it speaks of creation, sin, judgment, atonement, Commandment of God, redemption, perfection. All are well known themes of the Christian faith. Nevertheless, this doctrine is also strange. The cause of this, in my opinion, is that it incorporates the revelational work of God in an existentialist idea of God, namely, in the idea of God as history."[1] The last statement is not difficult to demonstrate. From what Loen himself writes, it is evident that the history of the Word takes place within God, for he writes: "God has condemned the sinner and abandoned him to death; yet He desired to bear the condemnation Himself and has Himself entered into death. This is the atonement which he has created."[2] "The atonement is that God has not remained unchangeable as the Eternal in the face of this event (namely, sin), but *has Himself willed to enter into an event*. Without this event, this inner movement in God, there would not be any atonement."[3] "The event in God is, in divine simplicity, that He bore the affliction due to the rejection of His love, and that He will bear this afflic-

[1] *De mens als historie*, p. 18.
[2] *De vaste grond*, p. 52.
[3] *Ibid.*, p. 54.

tion until the end."[1] "The resurrection is an event between God the Father and God the Son, a *human movement of God*."[2] "The redemption is . . . being filled with the Holy Spirit, Who prays, believes, and hopes for us, and loves us."[3]

The history of the Word is in Loen, the history of God. He has incorporated the idea of Existence in the idea of God and thereby radically denaturalized the motives of revelation. It is for this reason that Zuidema rightly characterizes his system as a *"Theistic Existentialism,"*[4] as a system in which revelation is accommodated to the thought of Existentialism. Even though this occurs in a genial manner it does not vitiate the fact that we cannot speak here of a Christian philosophy. Christianity has completely capitulated here to a system of thought which has not arisen out of Christian but humanistic roots.

A question arises which we cannot afford to neglect. Under no condition will Loen seek the starting point of philosophy in the self-sufficiency of theoretical thought. He repeatedly states that God is the fast ground or firm foundation of Existence, and also of knowledge. Without the Word of God we are not and cannot think. The exercise of science is also concerned with God, Who is the truth, the expressed utterance of all that is. And all knowledge is participation in the truth of all that is, thus it is participation in God. We are thus confronted by a thinker who has seen the insufficiency of the *immanence-standpoint* in philosophy and who is also aware that the hypostatization of one of the many cosmic aspects is an apostate religious deed of philosophical thought, which will not subject itself to the Word of

[1] *Ibid.*, p. 54.
[2] *Ibid.*, p. 68.
[3] *Ibid.*, p. 70.
[4] *Ibid.*, p. 17.

God. Therefore, as a pre-theoretical deed, Loen has chosen the starting point of philosophy in the *transcendent* principle of divine revelation. The question is whether or not this seemingly Christian system has *really* broken with the system of immanence-philosophy and actually accepted the only correct transcendent-standpoint of divine relevation.

This question must be answered negatively. In this synthesis-philosophy the motives of revelation are devoured by the non-Christian motives of Existentialism. Therefore, we are here presented with a *pseudo-revelation* of God and with a *pseudo-God* of revelation. For the revelation to which Loen appeals is not the infallible Word of the Bible that the Holy Spirit inspired. Revelation, for Loen, is rather a *speculative* idea which disguises itself in the mantle of Biblical terms, but does not have anything to do with the real Word of God, as a revelation of the divine truths of grace to sinners. Loen's idea of God is only human Existence projected into the essence of God, Who in absolute freedom posits Himself and projects His own history. Such an hypostatization is at bottom a religious deed of the human heart. However, it can occur only by means of theoretical thought. For the faculty of abstraction must lift human Existence out of the entire temporal reality, subsequently to deify it.

Loen chooses his philosophical starting point in the Word of God, a Word and a God, which he himself has projected with the aid of his abstracting theoretical thought. Therefore, by doing this he has not really broken with the autonomy of scientific thought and he remains caught in the immanence-standpoint. For: the standpoint of immanence philosophy does not necessarily imply a faith in the autonomy of human thought *in contrast to the remaining immanence* functions of consciousness. Rather, in accordance with centuries of development, it displays many diverse branches, ranging from metaphysical rationalism to modern irrationalist *Lebensphilosophie*. It also reveals itself in the form of modern Existentialism, which intends to break with the Cartesian rationalist *cogito* as Archimedean point, and following Dilthey substitutes *vivo* in the place of *cogito*.[1]

In summary, we must state that with respect to its starting point Loen's theistic Existentialism ought to be characterized as *pseudo-anti-immanence*-philosophy.

In spite of the difference in the conceptions of its various representatives, Existentialism, in general, must be seen as a development of Humanism, an offshoot of the *irrationalistic* branch of humanistic philosophy, and in particular it must be characterized as *individualistic subjectivism*. In this connection we must therefore ask: Is the system of Loen a form of Humanism? Are we here presented with subjectivism and individualism?

First, concerning the humanistic character of the system, we can conclude that if Loen's system is a branch of humanistic philosophy, it is not a part of Humanism which under the domination of the ideal of science is concerned with "nature." Rather, his Existentialism must be determined by the ideal of personality which must be qualified as *philosophy of freedom*. But, this ideal of personality is pertinently rejected and disqualified by Loen as a form of unauthentic existence, as a flight, from the authentic, that in the renewal of the present by the Word, stands before a decision. He says: "The common unauthentic yearns for independence in respect to time and the world, and it embodies its craving in the ideal of personality. It dreams of personality as being independent of the triviality of *quotidien* life and as being above convention and sensation. It thinks of personality as dominat-

[1] Dr. H. Dooyeweerd: *A New Critique of Theoretical Thought.* I. p. 16.

ing the world-time in a constant richness of its overflowing self. In this ideal the yearning for the authentic out of which it proceeds, is not understood: the personality is the conquering of the unauthentic, not through the authentic, but through the fiction of *ataraxia* or soul rest."[1]

Loen calls Existentialism, which views Existence as autonomous human Existence, a deification of man. Man is not deified in the azure heights of reason, or in the pressure of life, but in the despairing insurrection of being which wills to be itself.[2]

Yet all this does not remove the fact that Loen's view of man is actually rooted in a humanist theory of freedom, freedom from the law of God. For of the man in the state of justification, in which there is no longer any divine command, Loen affirms: "To show oneself as human presupposes further freedom. Without freedom there is no self. What does human freedom mean? It means that man can place himself in opposition to God. But he can only do this in accordance with the freedom of God, in which God has placed him in opposition to Himself."[3] Therefore, Zuidema writes: "This idea of freedom withdraws human Existence in principle from the law of God. The dialectical idea of law of this theory of Existence, in which human being simultaneously contains Divine freedom and creaturely responsibility, misunderstands the real Existence of man: his Existence under the basic commandment of love. . . . Human freedom in Loen's idea of Existence contains the same character that all Existentialism ascribes to human subjectivity: that of free self creation of one's own law and possibility."[4]

[1] *Ibid.*, p. 118.
[2] *Inleiding tot de Wijsbegeerte*, p. 181.
[3] *De vaste grond*, p. 9.
[4] *Ibid.*, p. 25.

Thus Loen's theory definitely must be included under the heading of Humanism, under the irrationalist theory of freedom of the ideal of personality. In this respect we can classify his system as *pseudo-anti-humanism.*

Are we also confronted here with a form of subjectivism? Apparently not, for Loen typifies human Existence as a being-in-the-face-of-the-Word-of-God. Our human Existence is determined by divine revelation. But what is subjectivism? It is that position in philosophy which seeks the law of our life in the subject. It does not start with a law which is given by God and which all creation, as subject, must obey. On the contrary, subjectivism starts with a part of creation which is, therefore, itself subject to law. Subjectivism elevates this aspect to the position of law and subjects all reality to it.

Existentialism has intensified subjectivism by elevating man in his Existence to the creator of law, thereby making him equal with God.

What is Loen's conception of the law of God? "God's Word of creation is no command but only a divine gift."[1] "In its origin, sin does not occur as a violation of this command, but sin precedes all command. In the history of the Word sin follows the creation and precedes commandments (law)."[2]

Does Loen not have a place for a command of God? Yes he has. A command arises after sin. "The command is a repetition of the word of creation, but now as an imperative."[3] But as soon as this command is given it is factually again rescinded. "The period of the command is the period of the forbearance of God. The time between atonement and redemption. There is no more com-

[1] *Ibid.*, p. 47.
[2] *Ibid.*, p. 49.
[3] *Ibid.*, p. 60.

mand for the redeemed."[1] "The command is thus only a command which is annihilated."[2]

From this it is sufficiently clear that Loen does not have any place for "the mode of being of the law of God."[3] In other words, human Existence is lawless and posits its own law and possibility. Consequently, we must qualify this subjectivism as pseudo-anti-subjectivism.

A similar case presents itself with respect to the question as to whether or not this conception is individualistic. Loen repeatedly tries to avoid individualism, for example, he states that in order to avoid solipsism we must emphatically maintain that God creates us in communion with Him. The individual is created as a member of a community; and the fall is *being-toward-death* by which everyone is separated and set apart by himself.

But in his ontology Loen comes to the conclusion that in the ontical sphere of *Dasein* (being-there) the terrain of Existence, there are many individual bearers, for each ego is an individual bearer. He writes: "The being-there, as a general basic-category, defines an ontical sphere; but this *ontical* sphere contains individual bearers."[4]

In other words there is no religious radical root of the human race, neither in creation, nor in redemption. The concept "community" does not have any *ontical* quality. It is only a collection of individuals. We must, therefore, conclude that this system is pseudo-anti-individualism.

[1] *Ibid.*, p. 60.
[2] *Ibid.*, p. 61.
[3] Zuidema, *Op. cit.*, p. 26
[4] *Ibid.*, p. 232.

PART II

EXISTENTIALISM IN THE
LIGHT OF CHRISTIANITY

PRELIMINARY SKETCH

OUR exposition of the various conceptions of Existentialism is now complete, but we are not ready to terminate our discussion. A Christian confesses a world and life view that is built upon the Biblical motive of creation, the fall, and redemption. Such a person cannot help but critically view all other conceptions in the light of his pre-theoretical commitment.[1] Every Christian ought to know why he must reject the systems of non-Christian philosophy. This rejection applies to the entire history of non-Christian philosophy, but it is especially applicable to Existentialism, as it lays claim to the souls of many of our contemporaries. Through its extensive literature it exercises a strong apostate influence on the life's tempo of the masses who have departed from the Christian faith.

The criticism offered by the Christian is directed and illuminated by the Word of God. The modern Christian

[1] Tr. note. The author is aware of the fact that in most philosophical circles an appeal to one's pre-theoretical commitment will be viewed as uncritical. However, as I have indicated in the Introduction, Mr. Spier is a member of a school of philosophy which believes that a truly critical transcendental critique of theoretical thought will reveal an intrinsic connection between philosophy and a pre-theoretic religious commitment.

For such a detailed critical investigation the reader is again referred to Dooyeweerd, *A New Critique of Theoretical Thought,* especially Vol. I. The reader who is not skilled in philosophy will be helped in his study of Dooyeweerd by another work of Spier, entitled, *Introduction to Christian Philosophy.* D.H.F.

is in a position to fulfill his *missionary task* by proclaiming his own answer to the needs of modern man. The Christian offers the many spiritually uprooted more certainty than is to be found by those who seek their escape in the newest form of worldly wisdom. The beliefs of Christianity are more certain and secure than belief in the abstract Existence of the man who despairs of all certainty and is threatened with destruction in the whirlpool of the total crisis of culture.

We must first give a clear account of the character of Existentialism if as Christians we are to view this philosophy critically. Secondly, we must seek to discover what *moments* of truth are contained in this philosophy. And finally, we must reflect upon the arguments which force us to reject Existentialism as a philosophy.

CHAPTER I

THE CHARACTER OF EXISTENTIALISM

I

ITS CHARACTER IN GENERAL

EXISTENTIALISM is a philosophy of reaction. A correct historical judgment of Existentialism must take into account the fact that Existentialism is a reaction against the rationalism which played such a great role in early humanist philosophy.

Humanist philosophy, based upon the religious *basic-motive* of *nature* and *freedom*, displays a polar tension between what we shall call the *ideal of science* and the *ideal of personality*. If a person absolutizes one of the so-called natural aspects (the pre-analytical) of the cosmos, in order to seek the total meaning of reality in this absolutized aspect, then a philosophy develops which is under the primacy of the ideal of science. This is what happens, for example, when the attempt is made to extend the method of psychology or natural science beyond its proper sphere in order to explain all of life's phenomena. The method of natural science is thus extended because of man's desire to dominate the entire cosmos by means of the power of his scientific knowledge.

The intention of the newly found ideal of science, which accompanied modern philosophy since Descartes, was to furnish man with unlimited power. But, when consistently applied this ideal of science had the wrong result. For was not man himself restlessly subject to the play of the natural forces that he intended to dominate or rule? Was man really anything more in the overwhelming system of the cosmos than a paltry atom or a bundle of sensory impressions? Was human Existence not completely determined by natural laws which dominate him? What remains of his freedom, of his personality and superiority to nature?

The ideal of science was, in its very foundations, a fruit of the humanist faith in man. Thus, this *science-ideal* called the philosophical ideal of personality into being, and sought the totality of meaning of the cosmos in one of the absolutized aspects of reality, for example, in the historical, ethical, or esthetic aspect.

In pre-Kantian philosophy this ideal of personality is the hidden root of the philosophy which was under the primacy of the ideal of science. However, the ideal of personality openly discloses itself in Kant's transcendental philosophy. Thus, Dooyeweerd writes: "In the final analysis the motive of freedom is the religious root of this basic idea and by its ambivalency it evokes the opposite motive of domination of nature. Before the rise of transcendental philosophy, this root still remained hidden under the primacy of the ideal of science, born out of the ideal of personality. The transcendental trend in humanist philosophy was the first to penetrate to the foundation of the ideal of science, in the ideal of personality."[1]

It would be a mistake for us to conclude that the primacy of the ideal of personality abolished rationalism in philosophy.

What is rationalism? Under rationalism we understand the conception that holds reason to be the law-giver of cosmic reality. Theoretical thought is deified. The laws of all aspects lie in reason, in thought. It is for this reason that all of reality can be explained rationally and can be

[1] *A New Critique of Theoretical Thought.* Vol. I.

intellectually comprehended. Something which is now a mystery can become logically clear if scientific method is consistently applied to it. When a form of philosophical rationalism has a metaphysical tendency to transcend the data of experience by thought, the deity itself is then identified with reason. When philosophy is exercised under the primacy of the ideal of science, rationalism appears in the form of absolutized special scientific thought, namely, mathematical, mechanical, biological, or psychological thought.

Rationalism can also appear, however, under the primacy of the ideal of science. In this case the laws of reality are not sought in absolutized special scientific thought, but in so-called transcendental thought. Thinking, concerned with the conditions of our knowldege in its apriori structure, is now directed toward the idea of freedom. This transcendental thought is viewed as the origin of the norms which determine the free human personality.[1] Existentialist philosophy is a philosophy of reaction, reaction against rationalism in all its forms. But this reaction remains enclosed in humanism, in a form of thought whose religious basic motive is a dilemma between nature and freedom.

Existentialist philosophy is irrational in nature. To be more specific it is a reaction within philosophy which is orientated to the primacy of the ideal of *personality*. This irrational philosophy is based upon a faith in the autonomous sovereign person of man; it no longer deifies cosmic law, but deifies a *subject* instead.[2]

Irrational philosophy of freedom has various forms. In the vitalism of Bergson the creating stream of life is hypostatized and proclaimed to be the origin of reality,

[1] See: Dooyeweerd; *op. cit.*, I Part III.

[2] Tr. note. A *Subject* is that which obeys or ought to obey a given law. D.H.F.

with its infinite sequence of individual forms. In Existentialism, we are confronted with a deification of the subjective human Existence, as an *historical* stream of experience.[1]

Van Peursen writes of the reactionary character of Existentialism: "This development is paralleled by an opposition against the autonomy of systematic reason which thought it could include everything within the cadre of logical concepts. We can observe this opposition in Romanticism and it is even more pronounced in *Lebensphilosophie*, vitalism. Instead of evaporating in the concepts of the withering glow of abstract thought, some decided to throw themselves into the full propelling stream of life. This movement was accompanied by an advantage in the sense that philosophy now concerned itself with the serious concrete problems of human Existence."[2] It is in this that Van Peursen sees the birth of philosophy that places Existence in the center of its view.

Zuidema also points to the anti-rationalist character of this philosophy when he writes: "Those who use the term Existence in the sense of this philosophy deny reason its primacy, supremacy, omnipotence and revelational character. They dethrone and disqualify reason. Existentialism is consciously anti-rationalistic. This anti-rationalism permeates its subjectivism, its theory of a broken reality (or nihilism), and its individualism. When Existentialism speaks of the subjectivity of man in a pregnant sense, then it means to say that the 'essence' of man is rationally unknowable with the consequence that it can never be the object of rational knowledge and withdraws itself from every description in a concept. For one of the constitutive basic characteristics of man is his freedom, more precisely his freedom of the will. Ra-

[1] *Ibid.*, p. 469.
[2] *Korte inleiding in de Existentie-philosophie*, p. 9.

tional knowability means exact insight and determination. To use it means a loss of freedom. Knowledge is power and to be known is to be powerless. Human Existence, however, is a source of unapproachable power and self-determination; it is not accessible to any analytical objectivity but is inviolably sovereign."[1]

Existentialism is also a *philosophy of crisis*. During the last half of the 19th century Western culture underwent a tremendous crisis. The question as to whether or not any certainty is to be found became an oppressive obsession. And it goes without saying that this crisis concerning certainty could not help affecting philosophy.

Stimulated by a dream of progress, the preceding rationalistic philosophy, whether under the primacy of the ideal of science or of personality, was optimistic in nature. Irrationalistic philosophy, in contrast, was soon to show a pessimistic face.

This attitude of crisis greatly increased the flood of pessimism, defeatism, and feeling of despair. Among its causes are the apparent insufficiency of science which cannot unveil the riddles of life and which is arrested by innumerable unknown and incomprehensible mysteries, the world wars, which have confronted us with the demonic background of human nature, the general collapse of culture, which raises the question as to whether we can still meaningfully seek the meaning of life, the mass movements of Communism and National Socialism, which clearly show that human life is not motivated by rational factors but by irrational tendencies which have a religious root, the impotence of man in the face of the great problems of life of anxiety and suffering, death and destruction, and the secularization of formerly Christian people is by no means an unimportant factor. Because of this latter cause, man has not only lost his certainty

[1] *Karakter van de moderne Existentie-philosophie*, p. 10ff.

in God and His Word, but he has also lost faith in any fixed order in life. Consequently, he has the experience that he is completely thrown upon his own resources and must seek final certainty in his own Existence.

Existentialism gives expression to the feeling of insecurity, anxiety, and gloom in contemporary man. Amidst the total cultural crisis, Existentialist philosophy seeks a final certainty to which man can cling in the absurdity of his Existence.

Thus, Van Peursen writes: "Man becomes conscious of his impotence and finitude and cannot embrace the being which surrounds him. Reality lies above and beyond the rational capacities of man. When he contemplates the inescapable and deep riddles of the destiny of human Existence, man is confronted with that which is incomprehensible and meaningless. Man discovers himself to be confronted with the threatening Other. And in this situation man again begins to inquire after the essence and meaning of his own Existence. He is driven on in this inquiry by the general disorganization of modern science, and is thus thrown back upon himself."[1]

And Zuidema writes of this *crisis-character* of Existentialism: "This philosophy cannot be exclusively explained as an internal theoretical development within an autonomous sphere of philosophy. It would be wrong to think of it as being free from outside influences. For in the first instance Existentialism is an exponent of a religiously founded development in the total cultural consciousness of the present time. With this fact is connected the great popularity of this movement outside of the sphere of professional philosophers. This tremendous influence is mainly due to the fact that Existentialism gives expression to the modern feeling in life of insecurity. Existentialist philosophy gives philosophical form to modern

[1] *Op. cit.*, p. 70.

man's defeatism, pessimism, despair, negativity and feeling of the meaninglessness and absurdity of Existence. Modern man feels thrown upon himself. He has been deceived in his Existence and feels no longer at home. He cannot grasp the meaning of life and seriously doubts the value of our culture and its future. He unflinchingly chooses to remain in apriori religious apostasy from God and consciously turns away from the revelation of God in Christ. He does this because he wishes at any price to maintain *himself*, against every Christian witness, in the confession of unbelief of pagan *self-election*."[1]

Further on Zuidema writes: "Existentialism interprets the consciousness of crisis of the uprooted Western European, the 'crisis of man' and of his lack of certainty. It gives expression to what lives in the hearts of thousands who no longer are anchored in God nor find succour in His Word and law. Thousands are estranged from a life with God and know themselves to be cast adrift in the middle of the world on a sea of despair. To their consternation, the world permits itself to be dominated in appearance only. It does not offer man any safety and cannot protect him against the fate of his freedom and the contingency of his Existence. It does not tell him why he is doomed to all sorts of failures. Man now knows that the very depths of his being are complete nothingness, perishable, and meaningless."[2]

Thus, as a philosophy of crisis, Existentialism is not only a sign but also a reflection of the time in which we live.

Existentialism is in the third place a form of *reduction-philosophy*.[3] What must we understand by this? Reduction philosophy is every philosophy which is guilty of a tremendous oversimplification of the problem of being.

[1] *Op. cit.*, p. 8ff.
[2] *Ibid.*, p. 14.
[3] See: Zuidema: *"De mensch als historie,"* p. 27.

It oversimplifies by overlooking and denying a part of the richness which God has placed in created reality. It denies the peculiar nature of various structures and seeks to subsume them under a false common denominator so that the diversity of reality is not given its rightful place and its various data are placed in a false light.

Every philosophical system which does not take the Word of God into account to the fullest degree must to some extent be guilty of such a reduction. The reason for this is simply that the general revelation of God in His Work cannot be purely understood apart from the light of divine special revelation.

Existentialist philosophy entirely rejects the revelation of God in the Holy Bible. Therefore, this reduction cannot be avoided by it. If the diversity of things and relationships are not seen in the place in which the Creator has placed them in the totality of His cosmos, then the richness of the creation can no longer be approached. The only path that is open is that which leads to a disastrous reduction and simplification.

In Existentialism this reduction has assumed alarming forms. We have seen that all existentialists have withdrawn themselves from the Word of God. As a result they will not hear of a divine law. In this form of reduction there is no room for any norms or ordinances which would dominate or rule human Existence and society. Man possesses absolute freedom and autonomy. If there is to be any question or mention of law or norms, they can only be the creation of man. And such an existential law has only individual validity. The autonomy of one individual is not empowered with the right to limit the absolute freedom of another.

This philosophy of reduction also lives in anthropology. The insight is completely lost that the human soul is the religious concentration point of all temporal functions. A part of these functions, namely, the lower (the body) are withdrawn from Existence and are reckoned to the "World." The remaining normative functions are united by the deified historical function into a self sufficient complex and are then exalted as a free sovereign personality.

In addition, Existentialism has no room for the structures of human society, nor for the religious root of society in the convenantal unity of mankind, whether in Adam or in Christ.

And in ontology, the theory of being, Existentialism digs a cleft between the hypostatized being of Existence and the being of the world which it views as something of a lower order, no longer united by the common tie of creation. In addition to this, Existentialism denies to the world its created significance within the total structure of creation. It makes this denial because it views the world only as a *pragmatic object,* an object of our human action. Our conclusion is, therefore, that *Existentialist-philosophy is an irrationalistic humanistic philosophy of crisis, in which uprooted modern man seeks to find certainty in his own Existence, which he has elevated to an idol. Needless to say this philosophy overlooks numerous veritable moments of the richness of the cosmos.*

II

THE DISTINGUISHING
CHARACTERISTICS OF EXISTENTIALISM

In the preceding paragraph we have tried to give a general characterization of Existentialism and have shown it to be philosophy of crisis and reaction as well as a *reduction* philosophy.

Our survey is not complete. We must still mention a series of typical characteristics if we are to gain a correct view of this movement. Not all of the characteristics that we have listed below play an equally active role in every individual existentialist. In each case the accent and emphasis is somewhat different. Nevertheless, if taken as a whole, they are adequate for our purposes and furnish us with a suitable characterization of this philosophical movement.

1. THE HUMANISTIC IDEAL OF PERSONALITY

Existentialism is in the first place a division of humanism. The latter is based on a belief in man and has as its religious *basic-motive* the motive of nature and freedom. Humanism embraces within itself thought which, under the primacy of the ideal of science, is orientated toward the natural aspects of reality. It also holds in balance thought that is based upon the freedom of man and is thus dominated by the ideal of personality.

Existentialist philosophy is sustained and nurtured by the ideal of personality. It strives to attain a philosophical foundation of the idea of man as an absolute autonomous being whose existence is characterized by absolute freedom.

In this connection it is well to observe that functions of reality which precede the historical aspect are considered by Existentialism as belonging to "nature," and this sphere of nature is abandoned to the ideal of science. Nature can and may be ruled rationalistically. Thus, Zuidema writes: "The way in which Existentialism speaks about nature betrays the fact that it follows Kant's critical rationalism and, for nature at least, accepts the humanistic view of science and reality. Existentialism's view of nature can only be understood in the light of the development of modern natural science and the rationalist confession that human reason dominates the sphere of nature."[1] And finally we must recall the fact that in the nihilist branch of Existentialism the humanist view of the autonomous freedom of man is undermined by a nihilist theory of man.

2. IRRATIONALISM

Existentialism is in its entirety strongly anti-rationalist. The essence of man does not lie in reason but is above reason. Reality may be ruled by reason in its lower regions. The sciences have their legitimate place in these spheres, but the mysteries of life, which arise from the existential being of man, cannot be fathomed or explained by rational thought. There is an unbridgeable cleft between problems and mysteries; it is this same cleft which divides super-scientific philosophy from science, concerned with the mere surface of things.

3. RADICAL SUBJECTIVISM

In general I have employed the term subjectivism as a partial description of philosophy which seeks cosmic

[1] *Karakter etc.*, p. 2.

law in the subject.[1] In this sense the various branches of rationalism can also be called subjectivistic in nature, for they elevate the subjective theoretical thought of man to be a law for the cosmos. In any case, rationalism still recognizes fixed ordinances and norms which rule reality in a lawful manner.

Irrationalist existentialist philosophy, however, has broken with this last recognition, at least with respect to its view of man. It teaches that human existence is not subject to any ordinances or laws which come from outside of man. Furthermore, this existential self can never become an object of rational knowledge. In the final analysis, existence is considered to be a law unto itself, the creator of its own norms. The subjectivism of Existentialism is a radical subjectivism.

4. ANTHROPOLOGISM

By this we mean that all Existentialism—including the systems that seek to discover an ontology—makes anthropology its central theme. This anthropology seeks real being in human Existence with or without any relation to the transcendent being of the deity.

5. EXISTENCE IS SELF-TRANSCENDENCE

The essence of man is sought in the hypostatized historical function of consciousness. Man is not, but he *becomes*. He is restless history. In each moment he exceeds himself in his free decision (ex-stase). He goes beyond himself. His Existence is continual self-transcendence, self-projection. Existence is being one's own possibilities. A person that exists is ever in advance of himself. This process ends with death. Only then can we say that in the totality of his possibilities man has become static factuality.

[1] Tr. note. This use of the term "subjectivism" is peculiar to Spier's own philosophy. D.H.F.

6. THE PESSIMISTIC VIEW OF LIFE

Existentialism is dominated by a completely different mood or attitude than that which was proper to Humanism in its original form. At its inception Humanism was extremely optimistic. It trusted in the superiority of man. The latter dreamed of attaining a utopia by continual progress. In an unrestrained manner Humanism approached a glorious future, full of self confidence and courage.

This optimism has now changed to pessimism, of which Existentialism is a philosophical expression. We now hear of anxiety and death, despair and failure, nullity, doubt, nausea, *éschec*, and guilt.

"Certainly there are many differences," writes Zuidema, "and I am inclined to think these differences are even greater than it is usually supposed, but in spite of the differences between the various existentialists, one feature is common to them all: they are all inclined to be somber and view the world and life in a dark and dreary way. Their view marks the destruction of all the hopes that had previously been extended in Christian and humanist culture. There is no longer any promise of progress. The most that can be done is to seek earnestly to stem the tide of the total crisis of the humanist conception of life. (The irony of the situation is that Existentialism has itself contributed to this crisis.)"[1]

This inclination to pessimism is also found in such people as Marcel and Loen, even though they are extremely far removed from the nihilism of Heidegger and Sartre. For we have written of Marcel: "There is no place for hope outside of the relation with God. Only despair surrounds us, against which we must unceasingly struggle in order to gain hope. We must not think we can over-

[1] *Op. cit.*, p. 7.

come despair easily, as it can also appear in disguised forms." And with respect to Loen, remember his disqualification of culture, which he considers to be idolatrous; and of religion, which stands under the judgment of God; and of our history, which is in need of redemption.

7. ARISTOCRATIC INDIVIDUALISM

Individualism is a term used to designate a particular trend in the theory of human society. It teaches that the origin of society does not lie in the religious unity of the human race, whether in the apostasy through Adam or in the renewing of Christ. Nor does this origin exist in a temporal social relation (e.g. the church or state) which embraces all other such relations. It exists, rather, in the individual, in personal individual Existence.

It is of course true that different existentialists attach a different significance and value to society. The one may view his neighbor as an enemy who encroaches upon his own freedom, and another may deem contact with one's neighbor as indispensable for true Existence. Nevertheless, both extremes are still individualistic because they deem the individual to be above society.

This type of individualism is, moreover, decidedly *aristocratic*. Real Existence is the possession of a few exceptional people; it never becomes the common possession of all. Only a few privileged reach this high level of existential Existence, in which in solitude man is placed before his own countenance. The majority, as *mass men*, are pulled down into the various forms of society.

8. THE ANTITHESIS BETWEEN AUTHENTIC AND UNAUTHENTIC EXISTENCE

All existentialist philosophy sets forth a specific theory of antithesis. This theory breaks with the postulate of neutrality in philosophy which holds that if anyone is unbiased and objective and does not allow himself to be influenced by preconceived notions derived from his general outlook, then he will necessarily agree with the results of "neutral" philosophy. He must agree because such a philosophy approaches reality phenomenologically and reads and describes only what it finds there.

This antithesis does not have anything to do with the Christian antithesis of belief or unbelief with respect to the Christ of Scripture. The Biblical antithesis is related to the religious duality in the human race, as a realization of man's eternal relationship to God. Existentialism, in contrast, bases its antithesis upon an individualist, irrationalist, subjectivistic view of life.

Existentialists distinguish between authentic and unauthentic Existence. Authentic Existence is the attitude toward life of everyone who accepts his own freedom and responsibility, is a law unto himself, and continually transcends himself through his own creative power. Unauthentic Existence, in contrast, is the attitude toward life of the quotidien mass man, the average man, the commuter who betrays himself by abandoning his own freedom, and is resolved in the world, subject to public opinion or to—externally arising—norms and laws.

This view of antithesis is in its roots nothing more than the opposition of individualism to universalism, within the limits of an irrationalist faith in personality.

9. THE SUPER-SCIENTIFIC CHARACTER OF PHILOSOPHY

This trait is a development of the irrationalist principle of all Existentialism. All existentialists make a principal distinction between science and philosophy. Science, in accordance with the humanistic view of science, is conceived of rationalistically and dominates natural reality by sovereign human reason. Science is limited to the pre-historical[1] reality, and this is called the "world" and can be rationally dominated as an "object." In the world one encounters *problems* which can be solved rationally. Such scientific activity takes place outside of human personality; it belongs to the sphere of unauthentic Existence. Science never touches the foundation of things or the root of being but remains necessarily on the surface. Real subjectivity, human Existence, can never be the object of scientific knowledge.

It is entirely different with philosophy. It is not concerned with problems, but with mysteries, with the great questions of life which can never be approached rationally but only existentially. These questions involve our inner self. We are affected by them in our very depths. Philosophy does not let our own Existence go undisturbed. Only philosophy whose essence is *existentiology* can teach us true self knowledge. Philosophy does not arise out of theoretical interest, but out of the existential vital needs of man, who knows himself to be insecure because he has seen his traditional certainties—including religion—to be illusions.

And this is the reason that Existentialism is called a world and life view and frequently pretends to fulfill the function of religion.

10. BEING IN THE WORLD (IN-DER-WELT-SEIN)

This motive is found in all existentialists. Human Existence goes far beyond the world, but yet it is in the world. The world is the sphere and object of our actions. Of course there is always the temptation to become absorbed in the world and thus lose ourselves in unauthentic Existence, and yet the world cannot be missed in the

[1] (See following p.)

process of free self-realization; the world is the means by which self-realization is attained.

11. THE CLEFT BETWEEN EXISTENCE AND WORLD

In spite of the being-in-the-world of Existence there is still a cleft between Existence and world. The two are divided from each other in principle and do not have any common root. Existence is free. It knows no other law than itself, whereas the world is the terrain of rational laws. The world is the sphere in which science, which must remain at a respectful distance from Existence, can express itself.

The human body is subject to the laws of the world and as factuality lacks the possibility of free self-development. Therefore, in view of this fact, the body does not belong to Existence but to the world. The existentialist does not understand by body the totality of temporal human functions which are concentrated in the soul. Rather he understands by a body a specific complex of some lower functions, which in any case are pre-historical.[1]

12. EXISTENTIAL TIME

Cosmic time which is created by God is reduced in Existentialism to an existential time, that is the time of man; not in the neutral sense of our clock time, the time of our days, months and years, but in the pregnant sense of the time of our anxiety, the time of our choice, the time which opens perspectives, the time of illusion and deception, the time which is death, but which also can become the time of life.

This existential time is composed of three dimensions, namely, the past as the factual, the unchangeable accom-

[1] Tr. note. Pre-historical is used here in the special sense of preceding the historical aspect in the cosmic order. D.H.F.

plished fact; the present as the moment of responsible decision; and the future as the unlimited sphere of possibility which is only brought to an abrupt end by meaningless death.

13. TO EXIST IS TO MAKE RESPONSIBLE DECISIONS

The concepts: decision, choice and responsibility appear in each system of Existentialist philosophy. The process of existential self transcending is accomplished by making decisions and a free choice in the seriousness of the present. Not only do the possibilities which we have today never return, but also the factuality of our irrevocable past crystallizes itself according to the decisions which we have made in our freedom. Autonomous man is responsible to himself for these decisions. He is his own law giver and lives in confrontation with himself, or with the Transcendent, which is hypostatized human Existence.

14. INTUITIVE SELF-KNOWLEDGE

All existentialists appeal to a certain intuitive knowledge, although the terms they use to denote it differ. Jaspers speaks of an *existential consciousness* or consciousness of being. Heidegger calls the most profound knowledge, *understanding*. Sartre favors the term *intuition*, and Loen speaks of *knowledge of Existence*. The object that they have in mind, however, is in each case the same. They all mean to indicate a certain self-knowledge which is not the fruit of discursive thought, but rather is directly given. This self knowledge accompanies Existence; it is an intuitive knowledge of one's own Existence in which knowledge and being converge. The content of this intuitive awareness of self is the certainty of our Existence as Existence, that we must become ourselves in self projection and self-constitution.

The preceding characteristics which we have listed are sufficient to typify the character of existentialist philosophy. These motives are not unrelated or arbitrary and cannot be arbitrarily replaced. For they are in their root connected with the humanist ideal of personality in its irrationalist trend. They are connected with the religious necessity of this secular thought, caught in the midst of an absurd illusory world, to seek a final point of certainty in the irrational depths of man's own Existence.

A person who bases his life upon the religious basic motives of Christianity cannot feel at home in the climate of Existentialism. And he should be aware of the impossibility of effecting a synthesis by accommodating Existentialism to the basic tenets of his Christian faith. There is a tremendous cleft between Christianity and Existentialism, which from the Christian point of view is a cleft which divides true religion from all forms of pseudo-religion, in which the secularized contemporary man of culture seeks his comfort.

The only way open to a Christian is to reject Existentialism radically and totally. The reasons why he must make this rejection must still be examined by us, but first, we want to determine what *moments* of truth are to be found in existentialist philosophy.

Chapter II

MOMENTS OF TRUTH IN EXISTENTIALIST PHILOSOPHY

I

THE QUESTION OF A *MOMENT OF TRUTH*

BEFORE we can answer the question concerning the moments of truth in Existentialism, it is fitting that we state what we mean by moments of truth in general. It is indeed superficial for a Christian to take the position that he can learn nothing from a philosophy which does not take as its starting point the Word of God, but a deified moment of creation. It is superficial to say: Is not a non-Christian conception completely false? Does it not distort and falsely present all truth? Can we learn anything positive from it, or can we only learn what we must not do? And is it not true that any value other than this negative one is a violation of the antithesis which divides Christian and non-Christian philosophy in principle?

If we want to speak in a responsible manner about moments of truth we must indicate what we understand by truth. What is truth? When one speaks of human truth he should not overlook the fact that four terms are involved. First, there is the knowing subject that wishes to acquire knowledge. Secondly, there is the knowable about which the knowing subject desires to get knowledge. Then there is knowledge itself, the possession of truth, that the knower has acquired about the knowable. And finally there are the *laws* of knowledge, in subjection to which the knower alone can acquire truth or knowledge about the knowable.

If it were the case that the *laws of knowledge* existed in the cosmos in isolation (that is, completely separated from all remaining functional laws, namely, the laws for all possible aspects of creation, and also separated from the highest law of life for human existence, the Word of God) then it would not be meaningful to even raise the question of moments of truth in non-Christian philosophy. For then not only would the antithesis in philosophy be abolished and the postulate of neutrality justified,[1] but then the non-Christian could acquire truth about creation just as well as the Christian. Truth would then only be the result of acute observation and correct thinking. But, it is not possible for the laws of knowledge to exist in isolation. No human act in life is isolated. Each act stands in a relation to the totality of our Existence in all its functions, and is related to the religious root of our Existence. Consequently, there are no isolated laws which are unrelated to the laws for the remaining temporal aspects and which are not influenced by the absolute divine norm of life, namely, the Word of the Lord. Obedience to the laws of knowledge in the process of acquiring knowledge is inseverably connected, not only with the remaining modal laws, but also with our re-

[1] Tr. note. The postulate of neutrality referred to here is the generally held position that philosophy and science are neutral with respect to any religious or pre-theoretical commitment. The author believes that a serious criticism of theoretical thought will show that science cannot be neutral with respect to philosophy or religion, and philosophy, in turn is also based on certain commitments with respect to the nature of man and the origin of the world, meaning, and law. Cf. Dooyeweerd, *A New Critique of Theoretical Thought,* and Spier, *Introduction to Christian Philosophy.* D.H.F.

ligious choice with respect to God. In other words, the knowing process itself is affected by whether or not our heart is open to the Word of God. It cannot help but make a difference if a person seeks his deepest certainty in a deified part of creation and thus lives in apostasy from the Lord.

And when a person rejects the Word of God, then this choice (which is religious in nature, although apostate), has a threefold influence upon his acquisition of knowledge. In the first place, such a person has a distorted view of reality. He does not view it in the light of the Word of God and consequently loses sight of the rich diversity of creation. He sees all of reality in the false light of a portion of the cosmos which he hypostatizes as something super-temporal. For example, if a certain school of psychology absolutizes sexual life and makes it the root of human existence, then it tries to explain all experience, including religion, as a sexual phenomenon. Or if one absolutizes the historical aspect, then he is not satisfied until he explains all experience as historical. When such absolutisms are made it is overlooked that human life is more than sexual life or history, and all experience is distorted to fit a preconceived schema.

This has a second consequence, namely, a *reduced* reality is retained. Only those moments are seen in the various aspects of life which are related to the part of the cosmos which has been hypostatized. All other moments are disregarded. For example, whoever considers the psychical aspect of feeling to be paramount in life seeks to reduce all the remaining aspects of life to a specific mode of feeling. Thought is conceived to be a psychical reaction which is based on logical feeling. Language is reduced to a linguistic feeling, and so on.

And the third consequence for human knowledge of this apostasy from God is that epistemology is also directed away from God. Where the heart is withdrawn from God the issues of the heart are also withdrawn from Him. If in a person's basic religious commitment he has chosen a part of creation as the source of meaning and serves this instead of God, then it naturally follows that his theoretical thought, in the process of knowing, will also be directed away from God. And from the Christian point of view Christ is the Truth, so that when He is denied our life is cut off from Truth and a lie rules our life and our thought.

With the situation as it is, the question can be raised as to whether it is still meaningful to speak of moments of truth in non-Christian thought. Is the antithesis not of such a deep and broad nature that no point of contact exists between non-Christian and Christian thought? Is truth not exclusively guaranteed to the person whose life has been renewed by the Holy Spirit? Is not the life and thought of the non-Christian wholly enmeshed in complete falsehood?

In order to see that these questions must be answered negatively, we must mention a very important point which we have previously neglected. The fact of God's general *conserving* goodness (usually called common grace) is of extreme importance to the Christian at this juncture.

When we speak about the consequence of sin for our epistemology, we have not spoken about the relation of the knowing subject to the law valid for epistemology. If it were the case that apostasy from God implied that it is impossible to obey the laws of knowledge, then and only then could we no longer speak of knowledge or truth in apostate epistemology. But this is not the case. God's common goodness not only maintains the structural laws for the temporal life of man on the earth, but a modal obedience to the laws and norms for human life is also possible in the temporal aspects of human experience. (The only exception is the sphere of faith, in which apostasy implies a loss of knowledge of God's revelation in His Word.)

A non-Christian does not have to think illogically. He can obey the laws of the analytical sphere. Therefore, he can discover the truth of various cosmic diversities. However, this truth is only a *detail-truth,* or a moment of truth. [Correct analysis is not enough.] In the special sciences we are not only concerned with obedience to analytical laws, but we also make a synthesis between the analytical aspect and another aspect.[1]

In the special sciences we can use moments of truth to greater advantage than in philosophy. In the latter our religious basic motive plays a more dominating role. In addition, philosophy must continually show the connection between all the temporal aspects. And it is of extreme consequence here to see that the law of the analytical sphere is connected with the remaining modal laws and with the religious basic law of human existence.

Thus apostate philosophy can never attain more than moments of truth. It can never place these moments of knowledge in a greater unity of truth. Truth in its broadest sense escapes it.

Nevertheless, we may not overlook moments of truth even though we must reject apostate philosophy if taken as a whole. Since God in His goodness has given us these moments of truth, we must avail ourselves of them and thankfully seek to benefit by the *truth-moments* to be found in apostate science, and seek to correct ourselves by seeing if our own view is in any way inadequate.

[1] Tr. note. The aspects referred to here are the aspects of the cosmic order. Scientific thought is [for the author] analytical and synthetical thought, in which logic is brought together with a field of investigation other than the analytical modality. D.H.F.

II

THE MOMENTS OF TRUTH
IN EXISTENTIALISM

WHAT moments of truth must a Christian acknowledge to be in Existentialism? In the first place we must appreciate the anti-rationalism of Existentialism. It is in truth incorrect to hold that reason is the law giver of cosmic reality, so that all reality is of a logical nature. But, Christians can go no further in the support of this negative position of Existentialism. For the basis upon which the rejection of rationalism is made is in each case different. The anti-rationalism of Existentialism is a reaction within the humanist *outlook,* an emphasis which is placed upon the humanist ideal of the freedom of personality, at the expense of the ideal of science and of the ideal of personality in their rationalist branch.

The Christian rejects rationalism on grounds which are basically different in principle. In principle a Christion must be opposed to every deification of a *cosmic given.* Not only must he be opposed to the hypostatization of human thought, but he must equally oppose the absolutism of any other cosmic aspect. It is for this reason that the Christian must break with both the ideal of science and that of personality in all their branches. A part of creation may never be elevated to the position of law-giver of the cosmos.

Whoever rejects rationalism, but makes another subject than thought the measure of all norms for reality, remains ensnared within *subjectivism* and thereby robs God of the honor which only properly belongs to Him as the sole law-giver in His world.

There is also a totally different appreciation of the logical aspect in Christianity than in Existentialism. The latter undoubtedly contains a certain disqualification of rational knowledge. What is a problem is on a lower level than what is a mystery. The lower reality of "nature" or of the "world" is deemed logically domitable. It is the object of rational knowledge and therefore is not free as it is bound to laws. This rational knowledge never probes deeper than the exterior surface of things; it is superficial and cannot reveal to us the essence of being. Human Existence, in contrast, can never be the object of logical analysis. It is free and autonomous and therefore withdrawn from the law giving power of reason. Even the principle of non-contradiction that A is not the same as non A, is not valid for human Existence. The criterion of Existence is just that Existence is never identical with itself, that it exceeds itself and is what it becomes.

In its appreciation of the logical, Christianity lives in an entirely different sphere. God posits His law for all creation, the basic religious law and the modal laws which are sovereign in their own sphere. And the logical or analytical is also one of these modal cosmic aspects for which God posits His law. Nothing which pertains to the cosmos is above law or posits its own law. Everything which is made has its *subject-function* in dependence on the laws which proceed from God. All concrete individual existence—whether of physical things or man in his temporal corporeal structure—function in all the cosmic aspects. Consequently, everything which is, has an analytical function subject to law. (This analytical function may be an analytical object function—the thing over which it can meaningfully be taught and concerning which knowledge can be acquired—or this function may be an analytical subject-function, namely, the man, who thinking about the knowable arrives at knowledge about it.)[1]

In this Christian view there is, therefore, no place for a disqualification of the logical, nor is there room for any exaltation of the logical that would hypostatize it and exalt it above the remaining modal aspects.

Existentialist philosophy is a warning to us to avoid the extremes of rationalism on the one hand and the pitfall of irrationalism on the other.

The second moment of truth that we encounter in Existentialism is the *rejection of the postulate of neutrality of philosophy.* Stated positively, this means that Existentialism recognizes that philosophy is based upon super theoretical prejudices. Existential thinking is thinking with the full personality, thinking that arises out of the deepest vital necessity of human Existence.

The rejection of this principle of neutrality for philosophy is pregnantly expressed in the theory of antithesis of Existentialism, the principal opposition between authentic and unauthentic Existence. (Objective science belongs to the latter.)

It is clear from the view of Heidegger that Existentialism holds that real philosophy is based on super-theoretical prejudices. "It is very possible that following the path of Heidegger's ontology, one can have theoretical insight into the character of authentic being-toward-death without one *ontically* being authentic being-toward-death. For *freedom-toward-death,* the acceptance of the nullity of one's own future and the Existence which proceeds from and is based upon this acceptance, is not dependent upon theoretical insight, but upon one's being seized by anxiety; and, vice versa, it is also possible that through anxiety one reaches authentic being-toward-

[1] Cf. Dooyeweerd, *Op. cit.*

death without having any explicit insight into all the structures of the *Dasein*."[1] And a little further on the same writer says: "Yet the scope of Heidegger's thought is clear. An intellectual knowledge of this ontology does not avail and lead to authentic freedom-towards-death. Only someone who existentially approves can also concur in his ontology."[2]

At this point our appreciation of Existentialism is also full of reservations. The sole point of agreement is with respect to the rejection of the illusion of philosophical neutrality. With regard to the positive statement of what ought to be included in the super-theoretical root of philosophy, there is an unbridgeable cleft between Christianity and Existentialism, for while the latter seeks the starting point of philosophical thought in existential experience, for example, in anxiety, Christian philosophy, in opposition to all immanence-philosophy, holds that philosophy ought to subject itself to the Word of God, which offers us the religious basic motives for theoretical thought. But, the fact that Existentialism has broken with the once so powerful postulate of neutrality, will perhaps remove in a broader sphere some of the prejudice against Christian thought, which has always taught the *unity of faith* and science.

Another point that we can appreciate as a moment of truth is that most existentialists seek to arrive at an ontology, a theory of being. In post-Kantian philosophy, philosophy is too frequently reduced to epistemology, because extra-mental reality, reality outside of human consciousness, is held to be a *Ding an sich* which is either unknown or unknowable.

Through the influence of phenomenology, Existen-

[1] S. U. Zuidema: *De dood bij Heidegger* in *Philosophia Reformata*, 1947, p. 62.

[2] *Ibid.*, p. 62 (the abbreviation is my own.)

tialism has broken with this epistemological reduction of the field of philosophical interest, and in this respect it shows more awareness of reality than many of its predecessors.

The appreciation of this can only be formal as far as Christians are concerned. For the ontology set forth by existentialists is in principle different from the ontology which arises out of Biblical roots. The former is entirely orientated to the idea of Existence, which rests on an extension of the historical function of nature. The latter, in contrast, is founded upon the basic motives of the Holy Scripture, in whose light Christian philosophy tries to explain the structures of reality, as they are experienced in our concrete experience.

We can also appreciate the fact that Existentialism gives much thought to *anthropology,* the philosophical theory about the structure of man and his place in the cosmos. This emphasis rests upon the correct awareness that, with respect to the rest of reality, human Existence is unique. Existentialism is aware of the fact that man occupies a central place in the great cosmic order.

But this is as far as our appreciation can go. For the anthropology of Existentialism is partially pseudo-Biblical. The anthropology of Christian philosophy, in contrast, takes the Word of God seriously with respect to what it teaches concerning the essence of man and his place in the cosmos. Of cardinal importance here are the revealed truths of the twofold unity of human existence as soul and body, the super-temporality of the soul or heart as the religious concentration point of all temporal functions, man as the image of God, the radical depravity of human nature, the conserving and renewing grace of God in Christ, and the covenantal unity of the human race in the apostasy of Adam and in the recreation of Jesus Christ.

The fact that Existentialism is predominantly anthropology is something of a stimulus to philosophy in general to labor in this field with full devotion, and it is also an incentive to Christian philosophy to seek a satisfactory solution to many unsolved problems.

Finally, we must still mention a moment of truth which is to be found in Loen's theistic Existentialism. In this conception the freedom of human Existence is in principle withdrawn from the law of God. Created-being, as such, is here emancipated from any subjection to a divine law. The commandments of God are present only since sin, and they are done away with completely in the atonement. Zuidema observes in this a "reaction against the reduction of the Being of God to the law of God." He says further: "This opposition is correct. The Christian may not disregard this warning and run the risk of living solely in the presence of the ordinances of God. An identification of God and His law works just as devastatingly for the Christian life as a reduction of the law of God to human objectivity. 'Fear God and keep His commandments' says the Bible. It does not say, 'Fear God's commandments and keep them.' Human subjectivity is not determined by a law which is isolated from God and which exists apart from and independently of His Will. Human subjectivity is determined by the Law of God and by the God of the Law. We live before the presence of God, of the living God."[1]

The meaning of the preceding is clear. Theistic Existentialism recognizes a real error which would subject Christian Existence to the Law of God, while evading the Law Giver whose sovereign will is expressed in the Law. In other words, man lives by a law and forgets God by abstracting the law from Him. Such a legalism can

[1] *De mensch als historie,* p. 27.

appear, for example, in replacing true piety, (the love directed to God and one's neighbor for His name's sake), by a set of principles which statically determine our lives. This is an undermining of the true spiritual life, in which is lost the dynamic power which the Church ought to exercise in the world through the living inspiration of the Holy Spirit. We ought to take this warning to heart.

Naturally, a wrong usage of the Law of God does not justify its elimination, nor does it justify the attempt to characterize created being as free from law. For every philosophy which rightly can be called Biblical must include in its ontology, the Being of God, and the Being of creation, and must also reserve a place for the being of the Law,[1] to which God has subjected all His creatures.

[1] Tr. note. The author uses the term "Law" in its broadest sense. It is not merely the ten commandments, but refers to all the laws by which God rules and governs His world. D.H.F.

CHAPTER III

REJECTION OF EXISTENTIALIST PHILOSOPHY

I

THE REASONS FOR OUR REJECTION

IN THE two preceding chapters we implied that we could only reject Existentialism in its entirety. In this final chapter we shall briefly summarize the general arguments which compel us to make this rejection.

1. First of all we cannot accept the *concept of Existence* as it is employed by existentialist philosophy. The kernel of its concept is always the deification of the historical function of human nature. Man is history. He is always in a state of becoming. He becomes what he is and he is what he becomes. It follows from this that the law which determines the *becoming* of human personality is created by man himself in his autonomous freedom. And, in addition, the remaining functions of consciousness of human nature are subordinated to or incorporated in the historical and thereby lose their sovereignty in their own sphere. Another consequence of this concept of Existence is that existentialist philosophy cannot have an eye for the supertemporal concentration point of the human person, or for the religious unity of the human race, nor for the constant structure which—according to the will of the Creator—determines our human Existence. The notion that human Existence is confined to limitations im-

posed upon it by creation is a thought which is unacceptable to Existentialism. At the very most the latter speaks of our situation as factual determination. But this concept of situation cannot be identified with any idea of structure, as the latter places us in normative spheres, whereas the idea of a situation merely places us in a subjective sphere.

As Christians we cannot accept this concept of Existence. This concept of Existence is defined as follows by C. A. Van Peursen, who is himself an existentialist, "Existence is the hidden root of our being, the concentration point of human *Dasein*, that has a specific vital direction and assumes a certain attitude."[1]

2. Another point of criticism is the *exaggerated function which existentialists ascribe to philosophy*. While there are individual differences between existentialists, all agree that philosophy is super-scientific in character. No existentialist speaks of philosophy as science without further qualification. Philosophy is not even science with a very special field of investigation. For some existentialists, philosophy is identical with a view of life. For others it is a scientific justification of their *Weltanschauung*, and for them a philosophical system seems to fill the role of a confession of faith; philosophy seems to take the place of a religion. This explains why we frequently encounter such religious terms in Existentialism as "repentance" and "grace."

It is obvious that at the basis of this view of science rests the pillars of humanism. For this reason it is unacceptable to us.

3. We must also point out the peculiar *idea of antithesis* which is propagated by all existentialists. Everything which cannot be fitted into the cadre of existential thought and life is stamped as unauthentic Existence. This

---

[1] *"Korte inleiding in de existentie-philosophie,"* p. 48.

implies an unbearable pride on the part of each existentialist, and it can only be viewed as a secularization of the absoluteness of Christianity. Moreover, all societal life, insofar as it is not made up of sovereign individuals, (this includes the Church) is completely disparaged. It is disqualified and called to repentance. "In order for the escape attitude of unauthentic Existence to be able to come to authentic Existence, it is indispensable that a change in rational insight take place. Thus we can speak of an element of repentance in Existentialism: existentialist philosophy appeals to the total person, it calls for a reversal of one's fundamental attitude."[1]

Christianity also teaches a theory of antithesis. And formally it agrees with Existentialism on one point, namely, that this antithesis is broader than our cogitative life because it grips the total life of man. However, in principle the Christian view of antithesis has an entirely different basis from that of Existentialism. The antithesis acknowledged by the Christian is not of a theoretical nature but is based on a division which exists between those who believe in and those who do not believe in Christ. Its reason for this faith is religious and stems out of a belief in the revelation of God.

4. We must also mention Existentialism's lack of a *unified vision* of the entire created reality. By exaggerating human Existence as Existence a cleft is made between the being of Existence and the being of the world. This comes to pregnant expression in the fact that Existentialism includes the being of the world in the schema of the humanistic ideal of science, whereas the being of Existence is to be approached only by way of the ideal of personality. Moreover, the attempt to bridge this cleft by means of the notion of being-in-the-world, is unable

[1] *Ibid.*, p. 49.

to eradicate the radical divergence between the two sorts of being. The totality of reality as seen by Existentialism cannot be comprehended in one basic idea of law. For if human subjectivity is the only source of norm and being, then the being of the world must be normless and meaningless in principle. Zuidema points this out in these words: "Now it is also impossible to arrive at another view of the background of human Existence after one has once accepted the apriori of Existentialism, namely, after one has founded law and meaning in human subjectivity. Everything which does not arise out of this Existence, must then be meaningless. Chaos is the polar counterpart of this exaltation of Existence. Also even when existence-in-the-world has as its consequence a limited domination of the world by the sovereign meaning-creating Existence, this domination still remains a domination over material which is itself unruly and chaotic. A vision of totality in which law and meaning find recognition in their universality and universal validity is excluded by this exaggeration of human Existence."[1]

5. We must note further that in Existentialism we have to do with a *secularization* of the Christian idea of creation and freedom.

If human Existence is deified, then it is consistent to ascribe to it creative power and absolute freedom. Thus man is held to be the creator of his own norms. He is honored as the being-absolutely-free. There are no external laws to which he is bound. He can make of his life whatever he wills and is responsible only to himself.

Existentialism openly or in a disguised manner denies Christianity. In any case the basic motives of the latter do not direct existentialist philosophy in any positive sense, but they do have a negative influence. The Bib-

[1] *De Mensch als historie,* p. 13.

lical motive of creation is secularized by ascribing the power of creation, which belongs to God alone, to human Existence, the deified creature. And God's sovereign freedom which does everything according to the good pleasure of His will, is also ascribed to man in the humanistic ideal of personality. All things proceed from man and exist for him.

From the Christian point of view only faith in the God of Scripture can honor Him, Who bears all things by the word of His power. God gives the historical function to man as His image bearer and this function, by controlled forming, brings the earthly creation to its completion in accordance with divine ordinance. Only the man re-born in Christ is free, but with a freedom which is bound to the religious and temporal norms given by God. The life in this true freedom is a life in the presence of the Lord, knowing that we owe Him an account for all our deeds.

6. In spite of all the glorification of Existence, Existentialism can never arrive at a true anthropology which gives a philosophical explanation of human Existence as it is given in our naive experience. The Existence of man is never experienced as a unity, a totality of soul and body. This unity of human Existence is theoretically broken up by existentialist philosophy into Existence or consciousness, and body, and this distinction is not merely a distinction but it is a cleavage. The human body is thought of as belonging to the world, which is separated from Existence by a cleft. This results in (a) the body of man is denatured to an independent complex of a number of lower corporeal functions; (b) Existence, man himself, is composed of a complex of higher corporeal functions which have their concentration point in the hypostatized historical function of human formational power; (c) there is no place for the soul as a super-tem-

136

poral religious concentration point of temporal corporeal functions; (d) the band is severed between the self, consciousness, and the functions of what is here called *body*, so that this body is alien to us and must be disqualified in principle; (e) the anthropology which results from all this can therefore not give an account of veritable Existence.

7. The *concept of time* which existentialist philosophy employs cannot do justice to cosmic time. It only represents a fragment of cosmic time because it ignores the numerous aspects of time.

Since Existence is a hypostatized human *subject*-function, existential time bears a predominantly historical character. Cosmic time, however, permeates all of creation and includes every earthly creature according to its modalities and structures. Therefore, it may never be identified with one of its modal expressions. Existentialist philosophy also reveals here that it is a reduction philosophy. Reality is theoretically impoverished and the richness of God's work is overlooked. To acquire a responsible view of time, philosophy cannot lack the light of divine revelation, for in this light not only is the temporality of all creation displayed, but our eyes are also opened to created reality which transcends the modal aspects of time in a religious sense.[1] And we are also aware of God Who in His eternal existence created time and holds it in His hand, and in Whom the meaning of all that occurs within time finds its ultimate completion.

8. Existentialism is not only foreign to the revelation of God in His Word, but it is also alien to the God of revelation. Some existentialists are convinced confessors of atheism which they propagate with all the vigor at their command. Sartre says: "There are two types of

[1] Cf. J. M. Spier, *Tijd en eeuwigheid* (*Time and Eternity*) Kok, Kampen 1953.

existentialists; the first are Christians. In this group I would place Jaspers and Gabriel Marcel who are Catholic. The other group, to which I belong, are atheistic existentialists. In this group are included Heidegger and the French existentialists."[1]

The completely Godless manner in which Sartre thinks is evident from his following words: "Existentialism is not only an atheism in the sense that it feels compelled to demonstrate that God does not exist. Our point of view is rather that even if God existed, that would not change anything. We do not only believe that God does not exist, but we think that the problem is not that of His existence; it is necessary that man regain himself and persuade himself that nothing is able to save him from himself, even if there were a valid proof for the existence of God."[2]

Other existentialists, in contrast, speak of God or of the Transcendent, but it is clear that this is not the God and Father of our Lord Jesus Christ but a philosophical God. This God is created in accordance with the example of human Existence, a hidden God, Who has not given unto us any revelation of Himself.

The existentialist philosopher, Loen, gives the impression that he wishes to construct his philosophy on the basis of divine revelation and wishes to confess the God of the Bible as the firm foundation for our life and thought. Unfortunately, a detailed examination reveals that in Loen's thought the existentialist motives of irrationalist-humanist thought have overcome and reshaped the motives of revelation. As a result, Loen has even projected his existential idea of man as history into the being of God, and thereby has abandoned the foundation of the

[1] Jean-Paul Sartre: *"L'Existentialisme est un Humanisme,"* p. 16. [translation my own. D.H.F.].

[2] *Ibid.*, p. 85 [translation my own. D.H.F.].

revealed Word of God, in order to remain in humanism, in a pseudo-Christian manner.

If apostate philosophy does not reckon with the God of revelation, nor with the revelation of God, then a pseudo-*revelation* replaces the Word of God. Frequently, anxiety functions as such a pseudo-revelation. For it enables the person who is fleeing from his Existence to be converted to authentic Existence.

9. Because of its apostasy from God and His Word Existentialism destroys the meaning of life.

It is not necessary to say very much here. It is, however, necessary to notice that this destruction of the meaning of life is not connected with the pessimistic outlook which dominates Existentialism. Optimism as such is no guarantee that the true meaning of life will be understood. If optimism rests on apostate motives of faith— such as was the case in the Renaissance and early Humanism—then such an optimism is essentially without any foundation and actually tends to obfuscate the meaning of life, which really can only be understood in the light of the Bible.

Existentialism does not have a monopoly on doing away with meaning. Rather the meaning of life is darkened by all philosophy which rejects the light of Divine Revelation. Yet there is a difference. In Existentialism there are conscious tendencies to withdraw from all the Christian influences still at work in Western Culture. There is a tendency to *radicalize* the fall by consistently drawing the conclusions of non-Christian thought. Ideas that originally were Christian are secularized and the origin of law is sought in sovereign man who is invested with divinity. This has as its consequence the fact that the meaning of life is less understood and man is left with the absurd. And this is the tragedy of the Judgment of God: "they have rejected the Word of the Lord, what wisdom is left unto them?" Philosophy is in need of a pre-theoretical religious commitment. If it rejects the Word of God and seeks its starting point in human sovereignty, it lacks the light which enables it to find any meaning in life. "Only in Thy Light, can we see the light."